# Cambridge Elements

**Elements in New Religious Movements**
Series Editor
**Rebecca Moore**
*San Diego State University*
Founding Editor
†James R. Lewis
*Wuhan University*

# NEW RELIGIOUS MOVEMENTS AND THE ROMANTIC SPIRIT OF MODERNITY

Stef Aupers
*Leuven University*

Dick Houtman
*Leuven University*

Galen Watts
*University of Waterloo*

Shaftesbury Road, Cambridge CB2 8EA, United Kingdom

One Liberty Plaza, 20th Floor, New York, NY 10006, USA

477 Williamstown Road, Port Melbourne, VIC 3207, Australia

314–321, 3rd Floor, Plot 3, Splendor Forum, Jasola District Centre, New Delhi – 110025, India

103 Penang Road, #05–06/07, Visioncrest Commercial, Singapore 238467

Cambridge University Press is part of Cambridge University Press & Assessment, a department of the University of Cambridge.

We share the University's mission to contribute to society through the pursuit of education, learning and research at the highest international levels of excellence.

www.cambridge.org
Information on this title: www.cambridge.org/9781009539265

DOI: 10.1017/9781009329033

© Stef Aupers, Dick Houtman, and Galen Watts 2025

This publication is in copyright. Subject to statutory exception and to the provisions of relevant collective licensing agreements, no reproduction of any part may take place without the written permission of Cambridge University Press & Assessment.

When citing this work, please include a reference to the DOI 10.1017/9781009329033

First published 2025

*A catalogue record for this publication is available from the British Library*

ISBN 978-1-009-53926-5 Hardback
ISBN 978-1-009-32904-0 Paperback
ISSN 2635-232X (online)
ISSN 2635-2311 (print)

Cambridge University Press & Assessment has no responsibility for the persistence or accuracy of URLs for external or third-party internet websites referred to in this publication and does not guarantee that any content on such websites is, or will remain, accurate or appropriate.

For EU product safety concerns, contact us at Calle de José Abascal, 56, 1°, 28003 Madrid, Spain, or email eugpsr@cambridge.org

# New Religious Movements and the Romantic Spirit of Modernity

Elements in New Religious Movements

DOI: 10.1017/9781009329033
First published online: December 2025

Stef Aupers
*Leuven University*

Dick Houtman
*Leuven University*

Galen Watts
*University of Waterloo*

Author for correspondence: Stef Aupers, stef.aupers@kuleuven.be

**Abstract:** Although new religious movements (NRMs) are characterized as diverse and unique, this Element analyzes the cultural logic underlying this apparent diversity from a sociological approach. Section 1 demonstrates that NRMs are substantially shaped by the Romantic counterculture emerging around the 1960s and its critique of churched religion, modern industries, science, and capitalism. Section 2 shows how these Romantic NRMs shaped the Western mainstream in the twenty-first century. Subsequent sections discuss the institutionalization of New Age spirituality in health care and business; the mediatization of modern paganism in film, television series, and online games; and the emergence of new NRMs in Silicon Valley that are formed around technologies of salvation (virtual reality, artificial intelligence, and biotechnology). The Element concludes that the Romantic spirit of the NRMs – once distinctly countercultural – has paradoxically developed into a driving ideological force that now consolidates and strengthens the machineries of late-modern institutions.

**Keywords:** NRMs, Romanticism, modernity, counterculture, spirituality, new age, paganism

© Stef Aupers, Dick Houtman, and Galen Watts 2025

ISBNs: 9781009539265 (HB), 9781009329040 (PB), 9781009329033 (OC)
ISSNs: 2635-232X (online), 2635-2311 (print)

# Contents

| | | |
|---|---|---|
| | Introduction | 1 |
| 1 | Historical Origins | 6 |
| 2 | Cultural Logic | 15 |
| 3 | Institutionalization | 25 |
| 4 | Mediatization | 36 |
| | Conclusion | 50 |
| | References | 53 |

New Religious Movements and the Romantic Spirit of Modernity  1

## Introduction

The "modern'" only begins to manifest itself when, in answer to the question, what is distinctively human? Romanticism replies not by referring to men's eternal capacity for reason and universal rationality, but, instead, to his creative originality, to his individuated capacity to feel and to dream uniquely

(Alvin W. Gouldner, 1973: 330).

Interest in New Religious Movements (NRMs) took off during the 1950s when the West saw the sudden and surprising birth of myriad and motley new religious groups. The 1950s proved to be an incubator of a veritable religious revival that culminated in the so-called counterculture of the 1960s and 1970s: NRMs as varied as the Unification Church, Peoples Temple, Hare Krishna, the Bhagwan movement, Church of Scientology, Transcendental Meditation (TM), the millenarian New Age movement, Wicca, the Church of Satan, and others became popular and appealing to many – particularly young people. Academics were quick to respond by introducing the concept of "New Religious Movements" as an umbrella term for this vast array of new religious and spiritual groups (Pokorny & Winter, 2018). Wary of the pejorative connotations of "sect" and "cult" (Barker, 2014) – both of which were, ironically, introduced much earlier on as neutral and technical concepts (e.g., Troeltsch, 1992[1912]) – sociologists of religion and religious studies scholars settled on the acronym NRM.

And yet, debate about the historical "newness" of these countercultural NRMs and the commonalities between them, keeps lingering. First of all, many of these NRMs were in fact not entirely new, but new renditions or mutations of established world religions like Christianity, Hinduism, or Buddhism. Examples include Christian-based NRMs like Sun Myung Moon's Unification Church (derogatorily called "Moonies"), the Children of God (now called the The Family International), and the Branch Davidians, as well as (Westernized) renditions of Hinduism, like Transcendental Meditation (founded by Maharishi Mahesh Yogi and known for its recruitment of the Beatles), the International Society for Krishna Consciousness (popularly known as the Hare Krishna Movement), and the Rajneesh Movement, founded by Bhagwan Shree Rajneesh (aka Osho). Given these historical continuities, it is often questioned how "new" these and many other NRMs actually are. Gordon Melton (2004: 73) observed in this respect that such NRMs with origins in Christianity or Hinduism tend to have more in common with these longstanding religious traditions than with each other.

Indeed, the undeniable diversity of countercultural NRMs that emerged since the 1950s has been a second issue of debate. Given that there must be thousands of strikingly different NRMs in the United States alone, and no less than tens of thousands worldwide (Laycock, 2022), generalizing about them appears doomed to fail. Even an impressionistic glance at the International Society for Krishna Consciousness, the Unification Church, Transcendental Meditation, Paganism, and the Human Potential Movement, reveals striking diversity in terms of doctrines, practices, and organizational forms. Some NRMs even seem to emerge out of nowhere without clear historical precedents. Examples are UFO cults in the 1950s, the Pagan Church of All Worlds (founded in 1961 and inspired by science fiction), techno-religions like Raëlianism founded in the 1970s and, more recently, popular fiction-based NRMs like Jediism, Matrixism, and groups exploring the spiritual side of *Lord of the Rings* (e.g., Possamai, 2005; Aupers, 2012; Machado, 2012; Davidsen, 2014). In ideal-typological contrast with "history-based religions," such NRMs can be understood as "fiction-based religions" (Davidsen, 2013) or "invented religions" (Cusack, 2010) and hence differ substantially from NRMs grounded in historical traditions. To complicate things even further, members of distinct NRMs tend to see each other less as fellow seekers and more as rivals in the religious marketplace, which suggests that looking for commonalities may be misguided or even inappropriate. It is therefore not surprising that Eileen Barker, sociologist of religion and astute observer of NRMs, comments that "to generalize about NRMs is a decidedly risky exercise; they differ from each other in almost every conceivable way" (2004: 94), even to the extent that "the only generalisation one can make without being shown an exception is that one cannot generalise about them" (2014: 20).

So what, if anything, do NRMs have in common, despite their differences? In the literature, two different types of answers have been given to this question (T. Robbins, 2004). On the one hand, there are the arguments that focus on *substantive* or *intrinsic* definitions of NRMs to point out what inherent qualities they have that unite them and set them apart from older, traditional religions. According to Eileen Barker (2004), for instance, NRMs are new and distinct from their traditional counterparts since their adherents are first-generation converts rather than members born and raised in a distinct religious milieu. This brings along a number of other features that distinguish NRMs from older religions: their highly committed memberships; the sharp boundaries between members and non-members; their leadership that tends to be charismatic rather than traditional or rational-legal; and their liability to internal change due to the fact that, inevitably, in a relatively short time span "newness becomes less new than it was" (Barker, 2004: 98). On the other hand, the demarcation of NRMs as a category is grounded in arguments that are *relational* or *extrinsic* and generally point out the strong, mutually constructed boundaries and tension between

NRMs and mainstream society. This perspective leads Melton (2004: 78), for instance, to the claim that religious tradition can manifest itself in churches, sects, or NRMs, with churches serving as keepers of tradition, sects dissenting from the latter within acceptable limits, and NRMs transgressing these acceptable limits, the latter's antagonistic stances "push[ing] them into contested space at the fringes of society" (2004: 73).

Bromley (2004) similarly observes that NRMs are deviant from the perspective of the established social order, pointing out that what defines them is indeed their lack of "alignment" with the "dominant culture" and "the structure and interests of dominant institutions" (2004: 92). In short, relational definitions of NRMs emphasize their tense relationship with mainstream culture and institutions.

Notwithstanding the much emphasized diversity of NRMs and their manifestation on a pluriform "market of ultimate significance" (Luckman, 1967) or "spiritual marketplace" (Cusack, 2010), we focus in this Element on the commonality of NRMs and their underlying cultural logic. Our main argument is that NRMs, despite their ideological diversity, are substantially shaped by the Romantic counterculture that emerged in Western countries between the late 1950s and 1970s. From the substantial or intrinsic point of view outlined earlier, then, we argue that the countercultural NRMs established between the 1950s and 1970s were a *religious expression of the Romantic tradition*. So we highlight how despite their otherwise marked diversity they are united by a Romantic worldview, critical of Christian doctrines and modern systems and institutions alike. Indeed, from the relational or extrinsic perspective discussed previously, it is precisely this "new," countercultural Romanticism that explains their strong tension with society and mainstream institutions. Yet, we demonstrate in the second part of this Element how Romantic NRMs, particularly the New Age and Pagan movements, have since the 1980s gained in popularity and have come to permeate the western mainstream, especially in the realms of health, work, media, and high-tech. In this process, NRMs lost much of their former oppositional, self-enclosed, and antagonist character.

## A Cultural-Sociological Approach to the Study of Religion

In unpacking our thesis in more detail, we rely upon a cultural-sociological approach that acknowledges the marked differences between distinct NRMs, yet focuses on the (counter)cultural logic that has shaped them and that defines their cultural commonality (see Bellah & Glock, 1976; Wuthnow, 1976, 1998; Tipton, 1982). In doing so, we abide by a number of methodological commitments.

First of all, we eschew moral evaluations of the "goodness" or "badness" of NRMs. As a result of their "deviance" relative to established religions and (as we will show) their shared countercultural, Romantic spirit – the existence of NRMs has long raised "moral panics" (Cohen, 1972; Goode & Ben-Yehuda, 1994; Richardson & Introvigne, 2007). A moral panic occurs when "a condition, episode, person or group of persons emerges to become defined as a threat to societal values and interests" (Cohen, 1972: 1). Irrespective of their particular beliefs or practices, NRMs have been widely perceived as threats, especially among more mainstream religious communities. Such moral panics have been commonly expressed in fears about brainwashing innocent children, sexual predations by charismatic leaders, drug abuse, and extreme violence. In many cases such moral concerns were well-founded. Indeed, some horrific events associated with NRMs continue to loom large in public memory. Think, for instance, of the 1978 murders and suicides of the members of Peoples Temple in Jonestown, Guyana, or the suicides by Heaven's Gate members in 1997. Such extreme events have led some scholars to express their moral disapproval of NRMs in general.

By contrast, in this Element we are not interested in the question of whether NRMs are good or bad. From our cultural-sociological stance we study their religiosity instead as cultural meaning, particularly as a form of *ultimate* meaning-making based on more or less clearly formulated theodicies of good, evil, suffering, and injustice in the world (Berger, 1967; Weber (1993[1963]); Campbell, 2007). In general, religious theodicies provide answers to existential questions about the ultimate meaning of life, which provide ontological security to people by explaining "why things are as they are" (Campbell, 2007: 166). Religious theodicies, expressed in doctrines, rituals, and social forms, are neither uniform nor stable. Compared to Western Christianity, for instance, Asian religions such as Buddhism or Hinduism formulate significantly different answers to existential questions and prescribe vastly different routes to salvation. Doctrines about the afterlife in Christianity, for instance, are related to Heaven, the human soul, or resurrection whereas Asian religions propose reincarnation, karma, and other solutions to the universal "problem" of death. Moreover, religious theodicies are never fixed: they differ across cultural contexts and change over time in intimate relation with broader, societal transformations.

It is from this perspective on cultural change and the dynamics of religious theodicies that we understand the formation of NRMs within the context of the counterculture between the 1950s and the 1970s. This was a period in Western countries during which the plausibility structures of "old," established (Christian) traditions, worldviews, and epistemic certainties were critically scrutinized from the bottom up, leading to widespread cultural change (Campbell, 2007). The Romantic NRMs that emerged since the 1950s, we maintain, both reflected and helped spur this cultural change. Following in the cultural-sociological footsteps of Max Weber, our analysis is ideal-typological, focusing on analytical concepts rather than empirical details. Moreover, it shies away from causal historical claims to focus instead on "elective affinities" between cultural forms. This approach, most prominently featured in Weber's classic work *The Protestant Ethic and the Spirit of Capitalism* (2005 [1904/5]), sidesteps simplistic historical causality or social evolutionism. Conceiving history as ultimately unpredictable, it is sensitive to the possibility – indeed, likelihood – of unanticipated consequences of social action (e.g., Merton, 1936). NRMs, we claim, may have been born in the rebellious counterculture between the 1950s and 1970s, in which new religious theodicies were constructed, but today their cultural logic is at the heart of many modern institutions, organizations, and mainstream media outlets.

## Outline

The elective affinities between the Romantic spirit and the NRMs that emerged after the 1950s are analyzed in two parts of this Element, each containing two sections. In part one (Sections 1 and 2) we analyze how the Romantic counterculture of the 1960s and 1970s provided the ideological foundation of the seemingly diverse NRMs that blossomed in that period. Section 1, Historical Origins, outlines the worldview of the Romantic movement in the eighteenth and nineteenth centuries – its critique of the Enlightenment, modern industrialism, traditional Christian religion, and its focus on (human) nature and expressivism. We then discuss its revival in the counterculture of the 1960s and 1970s. Section 2, Cultural Logic, shows how this Romantic counterculture left a profound mark on the ontology, epistemology, and soteriology of NRMs that emerged in that period.

In part two (Sections 3 and 4) we then demonstrate how the Romantic religious worldview of these countercultural NRMs – at the time considered deviant and subversive – has increasingly come to infiltrate the cultural mainstream in Western countries since the 1980s, exemplified most emphatically by the New Age and Pagan movements. Section 3, Institutionalization, demonstrates how central ideas and practices of the New Age movement have been normalized in the fields of health care (Complementary and Alternative Medicine) and business (Workplace Spirituality). Section 4, Mediatization, then discusses the increased presence of Paganism in novels, movies, TV series and videogames, particularly through the fantasy genre, and the emergence of new, technology-based NRMs in Silicon Valley. In the Conclusion, we finally discuss these remarkable and paradoxical processes of institutionalization, mediatization, commodification, and technological manifestation of erstwhile countercultural NRMs from a cultural-sociological perspective on modernity.

## 1 Historical Origins

Although the counterculture of the 1960s took shape more than half a century ago, it is by no means a thing of the past. On the contrary, it continues to live on, exerting its cultural influence in remarkably powerful and enduring ways. In 1981, Bernice Martin perceptively and presciently observed that

> Much of what was counter-cultural in the 1960s is now an unnoticed and accepted part of the givens of the 1980s, [as] the extravagant counter-culture of the 1960s ... familiarized the wider society with ... a range of expressive values, symbols and activities by showering them forth in their most extreme and dramatic form. (B. Martin, 1981: 23–4)

Indeed, "if [it] ever was truly a counter-culture," she observes, "it had certainly ceased to be so by the mid-1970s because its most characteristic methods and messages had been appropriated by mainstream culture" (B. Martin, 1981: 16).

Martin's observations are as true in contemporary times as they were in 1981. In fact, there is good reason to think they are *more* apt than at any other time. It is nearly impossible to come to grips with the vast cultural and social developments that have taken place in the West over the past fifty years without giving this tumultuous era its due (Houtman, 2008; Watts, 2022). This is recognized not only by academics, but also by political pundits across the ideological spectrum. Progressives and conservatives alike agree that the 1960s had a profound influence on contemporary society, even if their moral evaluations of this development differ radically. Progressives celebrate the era for paving the way for a more equal society, defined by increased opportunities for self-expression and self-determination for all, but especially for marginalized groups such as women, LGBTQ individuals, and ethnic and racial minorities. They celebrate the erosion of established traditions, the relaxation of rigid social norms, and the weakening of external authorities. Conservatives, in contrast, acknowledge these very same changes, but interpret them in terms of moral and social decline. We see this exemplified by former British prime minister and Conservative Party leader, Margaret Thatcher, who in her speech to the Conservative Central Council in 1982 declared: "We are reaping what was sown in the sixties. The fashionable theories and permissive claptrap set the scene for a society in which the old virtues of discipline and self-restraint were denigrated" (cited in Marwick, 1998: 4).

We argue in this section that the cultural innovations sparked by the counter-culture have indeed transformed the West and, most relevant to our analysis, its religious landscape. But from where did the counterculture itself derive? Was it invented from whole cloth, as many of its adherents were eager to believe? Or did it revive older cultural currents that had long lain dormant? This section maintains that we cannot truly make sense of the counterculture of the 1960s without acknowledging its historical roots in the movement known as Romanticism. We therefore outline the basic dimensions of the Romantic worldview, its revival through the counterculture, and the way it shaped a distinctly Romantic form of religion that animates post-1950s NRMs.

## The Romantic Critique of Modernity

How can we historically situate and define Romanticism? When Romanticism was born remains a source of controversy, but scholars agree that one of its first spokespersons was the French philosopher Jean-Jacques Rousseau (1712–1778). What Rousseau contributed to the Romantic outlook, most fundamentally, was the ideal of authenticity (Lindholm, 2008: 8). For Rousseau, humans are born unique and free, but are then stifled by the cultural conventions and social norms imposed upon them by society. In this way, Rousseau was one of the first to give voice to that distinctly Romantic feeling of modern alienation, born of the disjuncture between who one *feels* to be and who society *forces* them to become (Berman, 1970).

Romanticism has long fueled a critical diagnosis of modern society and its core ideas and institutions. For Rousseau, as for all Romantics, modern civilization spurs alienation. Because of this, we cannot simply consider Romanticism as an a-historical philosophical idea born in the abstract, but need to place it in its historical and cultural context.

Romanticism first developed in England, France, and Germany during the eighteenth and nineteenth centuries as a reaction to the Enlightenment, opposing its theoretical foundations as well as their practical ramifications in everyday life. The key targets of romantic critique were rationalism, modern science, industrialism, and the sense of alienation these were seen to generate. The modern natural sciences, Romantics asserted, might well provide a more objective understanding of how the world actually works, but they simultaneously turn an animated world full of wonder and enchantment into a cold mechanistic universe dominated by meaningless causal relationships. They blamed particularly Isaac Newton's (1643–1727) paradigm-changing scientific discoveries for this "mechanization," feeling strongly that "his philosophy had 'clipped an angel's wings,' disenchanting the world and reducing all life to the status of a machine" (Campbell, 1987: 181). The rigid emphasis in science on reason, empiricism, facts, and objectivity was condemned as an irreparable threat to vital subjective human faculties such as imagination, personal intuition, feeling, and experience. Confronted with modern industrialism halfway through the eighteenth century – pioneered by technology and giving rise to mass production – Romantics also fiercely critiqued modern factories. In his famous poem *Jerusalem* (1998 [1804]), William Blake referred to these as "dark Satanic mills" substantially undermining the quality of human handcraft, polluting the "green" natural landscape with their smoking chimneys, and producing a general sense of alienation. In the Romantic discourse, then, "nature" – not least human nature – purity, and authenticity were celebrated as intrinsically sacred, juxtaposed to the disturbing profanities of modern society. In nature, Rousseau proposed, humans are free to be who they are, to express their "true" selves and to live in harmony with one another and the natural world alike, whereas in modern society they are forced to repress their basic needs and desires. For the Romantic, then, the birth of "the modern" is akin to the biblical Fall from Eden.

The Romantic movement expressed these themes in art, poetry, architecture, and philosophy. Across the works of disparate Romantic writers and artists – Jean-Jacques Rousseau, Percy Bysshe Shelley, William Blake, Samuel Taylor Coleridge, Novalis (aka Georg Philipp Friedrich), or Victor Hugo – we find a rebellion against the Enlightenment's emphasis on science, industrialism, rationalism, and formal harmony, in favor of the natural world, imagination, and self-expression (Trilling, 1971). Central to Romanticism is what philosopher Charles Taylor (1989) refers to as "expressivism," the idea that the principal goal of life is realizing the distinctive and original potentiality that each and every individual has within them. The assumption that there is something natural, unique, and authentic within the deeper layers of the self that needs to be discovered and expressed in everyday life is, indeed, at the heart of Rousseau's pioneering work. It is the key to Romantic salvation in and from the modern world as well as a potential source of re-enchantment.

Moreover, the early Romantics took an ambivalent stance toward traditional religion. They were critical of secularism, maintaining that secular scientists preached nihilistic formulas that depicted the world as mechanistic, reducing it to an object of study and robbing it of its mystery and meaning. And yet, they also charged traditional Christian (particularly "churched") religion with preaching formal doctrines insisting on obedience, conformity, and thereby obstructing vital feelings of transcendence, ecstasy, supernatural experience, and spiritual enchantment. Dismissing rationalist secularism *and* churched-doctrinal Christianity alike, the Romantics deemed alternative epistemological venues pivotal to imbue the world with ultimate meaning once again. Historian Peter Gay summarizes this Romantic ambition as follows:

> The prophets, poets, and propagandists of the nineteenth-century quest for the naked heart were the romantics. They explored its possibilities and complicated its outlines; they refined its vocabulary and more or less unwittingly shaped the bourgeoisie's perception of the self for decades ahead. The stakes were high: leading romantics saw it as their historic mission to re-enchant the world. They felt an urgent need to restore the sense of wonder and mystery that eighteenth-century deists, skeptics, and atheists – Voltaire and Hume and Holbach and their fellow mutineers against faith – had attempted to erase with their bloodless scientism, impious insults, and shallow witticisms. The Enlightenment had, romantics charged, damaged the inner life almost beyond repair. Theirs was a brave effort. Disenchanted with disenchantment, they worked to undo the secularization of the world that had been the dismal accomplishment of their father's generations. (Gay, 1995: 37)

Secularism, or what Max Weber (2005 [1904/5]) called the "disenchantment of the world" through rationalism, science, and industry, thus constituted the principal problem in the life-world of the early Romantics. How did they cope with this challenge? Romantics found solace in art and artistic expression. While immersed in literature, poetry, painting, and other aesthetically pleasing realms of beauty, they could temporarily "suspend their disbelief," as Samuel Coleridge (1834: 175) famously argued. Indeed, Safranski (2014) goes so far as to propose that Romanticism was essentially a continuation of religion by aesthetic means. At a more fundamental level, however, the Romantics considered artistic expression the inevitable outcome of a natural, authentic, and god-like source of creativity lying within every person. The underlying assumption was that modern individuals needed to shake off the limiting and alienating bonds that entrap them, so as to reconnect with their unique, creative, free selves to find ultimate meaning, re-unite with their (human) nature, and re-enchant the world. What distinguished the Romantic theodicy from others, Colin Campbell summarizes,

> was the fact that primary emphasis was placed upon the characteristic of creativity ... whilst the divine itself was no longer represented as a named, personal God, but as a supernatural force, which, whilst present throughout the natural world, also existed within each individual in the form of a unique and personalized spirit; that of his "genius." (Campbell, 1987: 182)

This, then, is the Romantic theodicy developed in the eighteenth and nineteenth centuries: a substantial critique of modern society, complemented by the celebration of (human) nature and the ideal of self-expression. This Romanticism was not a temporary hiccup in history. It shaped, to quote Gay (1995: 37), once again, "the bourgeoisie's perception of the self for decades ahead," and transformed modern culture in many respects (e.g., Taylor, 1989), not least by giving rise to the NRMs in the bosom of 1960s counterculture.

## The Romantic Counterculture

Early Romanticism remained largely confined to artistic and intellectual elites, manifesting itself primarily in art, music, literature, poetry, painting, and philosophical reflection. Since then, however, it has become popular in and through various social and cultural movements in the West, most notably in historical periods of rapid social and technological change. Indeed, given its critical ideological positioning against tradition *and* modernity, Romanticism historically played an important role in many revolutions of the masses against those in power. This is exemplified by the French revolution at the end of the eighteenth century, in which the writings of Rousseau and other distinguished Romantics explicitly fueled protests against the *ancien régime* and motivated a collective uprising for equality and individual freedom. On the other end of the political spectrum, Romanticism was appropriated by the Nazis in Germany from 1933 onwards, among others, to legitimate the "natural" (and hence "superior") order of the German nation state and the Aryan race (Safranski, 2014). Close to the topic of religion were the mutual influences of Romanticism and the long-standing Western esoteric tradition (Hanegraaff, 1996: 415–21), both part and parcel of a "Counter-Enlightenment" in modern culture. Esotericism constitutes a "Romantic religion" *par excellence*, rooted as it is in a religious naturalism that foregrounds correspondences that claim that "everything is connected" while taking humans to be essentially spiritual beings (420). Modern esoteric movements in the nineteenth century, most notable Blavatsky's Theosophical Society (founded in 1875), Spiritualism, the New Though Movement and their later offshoots, have done much to popularize the Romantic worldview (Hammer, 2001).

Overall, then, Romanticism has taken many forms in Western society over the last two centuries, providing ideological fuel for revolt, protest, and revolution against established traditions and the ailments of modernity. Its countercultural potential manifested once again when it democratized and popularized among the young "protest generation" of baby boomers after WWII. Particularly during the 1960s, the Romantic critique of the rationalized modern order merged with liberal political ideals on a grand scale, giving life to an "expressive revolution" (Parsons & Platt, 1973; see also B. Martin, 1981; Watts, 2022). Notwithstanding the diversity of its young participants – ranging from political protesters and anarchists to Bohemians experimenting with mind-expanding drugs, psychedelics, and spirituality – the continuity of the counterculture with the Romantic tradition is widely acknowledged. "Considered as a group of people who are distinguished by a particular way of life and the values and beliefs that it embodies," Colin Campbell (2007: 188) asserts, "the counterculture of the 1960s can ... probably best [be] understood as the social expression of Romanticism." It animated a liberal democratic tradition of "expressive individualism" (Bellah et al., 1985) that inspired radical lifestyle experimentation, sparked mass protest, and powered a host of social and political movements (Berman, 1970). One of the most remarkable features of the countercultural critique in that period is that it was neither voiced by the industrial working class, nor did it single out capitalist exploitation and economic inequality as modernity's principal shortcomings. Instead, middle-class youth served as its principal carriers (Inglehart, 1977), championing what was, in effect, the same critique of modernity that earlier Romantics had articulated (Boltanski & Chiapello, 2007).

Countercultural Romanticism directly targeted traditional Christian religion, challenging its institutional structures and rejecting church dogmas and doctrines. Counterculturalists rejected the doctrine of original sin or human depravity in favor of a Romantic conception of human benevolence (Woodhead, 1993). While this critical stance vis-à-vis traditional Christian religion may at first glance appear consistent with widely accepted sociological notions of modernization and secularization, the matter is more complex than this. Sociological orthodoxy attributes the loss of authority of traditional religion and morality to an increased authority of science, technology, and rationality (Wilson, 1985). In this understanding, rationalization allegedly gives rise to a warfare of science with theology (White, 1960) or a religion/science conflict (Sappington, 1991), with "religion's inevitable demise ... framed in terms of physical science discoveries that expose the fallacies of religious superstitions and technological progress that reduces the appeal of religious promises" (Iannaccone, Stark, & Finke, 1998: 384). Yet, a crucial feature of the Romantic counterculture of the 1960s is that it was not only critical of traditional Christianity, but equally of the authority of science or, more generally, of "an ideology that places a high value on rationality, calculation and efficiency," critiquing the latter in the name of "an ideology of self-fulfillment, spontaneity and experiential richness" (B. Martin, 1981: 17, 18). Thus, while the Romantic spirit of the counterculture critiqued the Christian churches, it was arguably even more of a challenge to what B. Martin (1981: 21) calls "the instrumental enclave," that is, modern science and the technologized systems it sustains. As she puts it,

> What [the counterculture] "countered" was not so much traditional cultural values as the contrasting hemisphere of instrumentality and power, work and

> politics. The counterculture ... pushed Romantic individualism to ever more extreme lengths in contra-distinction to the bureaucratic and bourgeois individualism of the instrumental enclave. (B. Martin, 1981: 21)

This countercultural Romanticism is perhaps best captured by Theodore Roszak's book *The Making of a Counter Culture* (1969), immensely popular in countercultural circles, and itself a countercultural pamphlet as much as a social-scientific analysis. The Enlightenment dream of science- and rationality-led processes of liberation and emancipation, Roszak contended, had resulted in dominance by scientifically trained specialists, themselves mere cogs in a rationalized system on a "relentless quest for efficiency, for order, for ever more extensive rational control" (Roszak, 1969: 21). Due to its strictly formal rationality, this "technocracy" was rejected as void of meaning and a threat to morality, human freedom, and opportunities for personal growth. It was seen as instrumentalizing human beings and manipulating them into conformity. "'The System'," Roszak reprovingly observed (1969: 17), "tries to make us believe that we are 'free' and 'happy'."

In addition to utilizing Roszak's book, young countercultural critics drew much of their intellectual ammunition from the philosophers and sociologists of the Frankfurt School, who brought out basically identical arguments in a more theoretically and philosophically sophisticated manner. In *Dialectics of Enlightenment* – a telling title – Theodor Horkheimer and Max Adorno (2002 [1944]) claimed that reason's reduction to mere instrumentality and calculability had transformed it from an emancipatory force into an essentially oppressive one. Contrary to the glowing promises of the Enlightenment, people in the West had not at all ended up living free and happy lives in tolerant, democratic societies. They were merely made to believe that they did. Horkheimer and Adorno blamed especially what they called the "culture industries" of film, radio, and advertising for keeping the public in a complacent state of unconsciousness that veils modern capitalism's manipulative mechanisms and seduces individuals into mistaking their alienation for happiness. In addition, the Frankfurt writers accused modern positivist science of mystifying these wrongs with the cloak of clarity through its strict empiricism, bordering on "fact fetishism." Limiting itself to the study of actually existing reality, understood as "what is," it neglected the equally, if not more, important realm of "what is not, yet could be." In the eyes of the Frankfurt school, a utopianism that foregrounded how the actually existing world could be transformed in ways that expand human freedom and liberate humans from their sorry state of alienation, was more important than narrowly conceived empirical social science (Horkheimer & Adorno, 2002[1944]; see also Marcuse, 1964).

Motivated by influential ideas such as these, members of the counterculture critiqued positivist science as a handmaiden of "technocracy" which forced people into slave-like existences (e.g., Roszak, 1969; Horkheimer & Adorno, 2002[1944]). By accusing rationalist science of being a status-quo-serving conservative politics in disguise, they dismissed positivist claims of neutrality and objectivity. Overall, then, the upsurge of the Romantic counterculture of the 1960s not only dismissed traditional Christian religion for being overly dogmatic and reducing modern humans to obedient role-playing puppets; it also criticized modern science and its rationalist technocratic offshoots on precisely the same grounds. The alternative to this deeply felt alienation was found in a Romantic return to (human) nature and an ethics of self-expression that animated initiatives ranging from secular politics, wild anarchistic groups, musical subcultures, experiments with drugs to, indeed, the formation of New Religious Movements.

## Religious Change since the Counterculture

Colin Campbell (2007: 213) refers to the 1960s counterculture as "the hinge of modern history" – a transformative period that can be compared to the Renaissance, the French Revolution, and other historical periods in which dissatisfaction with the status quo and the establishment led to rapid cultural change. It is now widely acknowledged that Romantic countercultural values, not least personal authenticity and self-expression – "being your true self" – have become central to contemporary culture, even invading domains such as work and consumption. The corporate world, for instance, witnessed a shift from hierarchical and bureaucratic organizations to flatter ones, with self-directing, flexible, and proactive employees becoming the new norm (Boltanski & Chiapello, 2007; Watts & Houtman, 2022). Meanwhile, self-help books no longer advise junior entrants into the labor market to adapt to work organizations' demands, but rather encourage them to follow their personal passion and seek out opportunities for personal growth (De Keere, 2014). In consumer culture, authenticity has become the holy grail (Gilmore & Pine, 2007), as can be seen in the contemporary appeal of vintage clothing and antique furniture (Veenstra & Kuipers, 2013); organic foodstuffs (Ward, Coveney, & Henderson, 2010); traditional craftsmanship, and artisanal production (Ocejo, 2017). Reflecting on these changes in consumer culture, the historian and journalist Thomas Frank writes

> Now products exist to facilitate our rebellion against the soul-deadening world of products, to put us in touch with our authentic selves, to distinguish

us from the mass-produced herd, to express our outrage at the stifling world of economic necessity. (Frank, 1998: 229)

Of utmost importance for this Element is how the Romantic upsurge of the 1960s changed the religious domain by animating a diversity of NRMs. It did so because the Romantic worldview rejected and undermined both principal pillars of Western society – modern science, rationalism, and reason, along with institutional "churched" Christianity and traditional religious beliefs. Even though Romanticism cannot and should not be understood as a religious movement in and of itself, the Romantic critique of modernity and the myriad experiments with alternative forms of meaning-making that emerged in the nineteenth century – from Transcendentalism and Theosophy to New Thought and Spiritualism – provided a cultural blueprint for middle-class young adults in the 1960s. That is, Romanticism nourished a deep hunger for new types of religion and the emergence of countless new, non-institutionalized religious initiatives in what has been called an open "market of ultimate significance" (Luckmann, 1967: 99).

From a broader sociological perspective, this rise of new types of religion shows that the decline of Christian religion is not the end of religion as such but coincides with a process of religious transformation (Luckmann, 1967; Watts and Houtman, 2024). Secularization, in other words, can be understood as a "self-limiting process" that "also stimulates religious innovation" (Stark & Bainbridge, 1985: 2). Writing about the United Kingdom, historian Callum Brown notes that the period between 1956 and 1973 – "the long sixties," as he calls it – accounts for no less than half of the total decline in British Christianity in the twentieth century: "an unremitting decline in membership, communicants, baptisms, and religious marriage which, at the start of the third millennium, shows no sign of bottoming out" (Brown, 2001: 188). The patterns Brown observes for the United Kingdom can be generalized to Western countries (Norris & Inglehart, 2004), even though there are obviously cross-national differences, with especially the United States long considered an exceptional case (see, however, Voas & Chaves, 2016). And yet, the massive exodus from the Christian churches in the 1960s and 1970s, particularly in Western Europe, did not mark the end of religion. Many of the baby boomers that left their childhood religions behind ended up undertaking a spiritual quest for new types of religion beyond the institutional control of church and sect. As we will discuss in the next section, the NRMs that emerged in this era indeed had a marked Romanticism in common, despite their otherwise clear diversity and their roots in traditions ranging from esotericism, Buddhism, and Hinduism to nontraditional forms of Christianity.

## 2 Cultural Logic

NRMs differ in terms of specific beliefs, organizational dynamics, sociopolitical orientations, and ideological heritage. At first glance it seems hard to find commonality between those with roots in Buddhist or Hinduist worldviews, like Transcendental Meditation, the Bhagwan, or Hare Krishna movements; those that boast nontraditional forms of Christianity, such as Pentecostalism or charismatic movements; and those rooted in Western esoteric movements like paganism, New Age, and the Human Potential Movement. Yet, we argue in this section that these NRMs do nonetheless have a marked Romanticism in common, a cultural similarity that has often been neglected by focusing on their differences thereby inhibiting theoretical generalization. This is why we discuss the three principal ideal-typological dimensions of this Romanticism in this section. First, we delineate a *religious ontology* that breaks with dualism and posits the existence of an immanent spirit or divine life force in the natural world. Second, we identify a *religious epistemology* that problematizes "faith" and "reason" as avenues to truth and holds that access to spiritual truth necessitates direct, personal and lived experience, or "gnosis." And third, there is a *religious soteriology* which holds that humans can be "saved" by achieving freedom through self-expression and realizing one's authentic self.

## Religious Ontology

That the 1960s counterculture unleashed a tidal wave of spiritual yearning beyond the Christian church is a central argument in Colin Campbell's *The Easternization of the West* (2007). A Weberian sociologist of religion, Campbell contends that this postwar era reflected a crisis of meaning, because the existential needs of the baby boom generation could not be met by the mainstream churches and their long-standing, institutionalized theodicies in Western societies. In turn, young seekers were craving novel meaning systems that could satisfy their spiritual hunger, ultimately embracing one or other Romantic type of religion. The result was a large-scale generational shift from the *materialistic dualism* that had long been the Western default to an Asian-style *metaphysical monism*, a process that Campbell (2007: 60) has dubbed "Easternization." Put another way, the radically transcendent and otherworldly God of the Puritans – which Weber saw as pivotal to the birth of modernity – was forcefully rejected, in favor of a more immanent and omnipresent conception of the divine.

In some cases, this meant a direct turn to Asian religions that are, according to Campbell (2007), more animistic, pantheistic, and polytheistic than Western ones. For instance, many countercultural baby boomers became fascinated with Hinduism in the 1960s. Some of them took off to India to find a guru and live in an ashram, while others stuck to the West and embraced an imported movement from Asia. One of the most popular of these was TM (in full: Transcendental Meditation and the Spiritual Regeneration Movement), founded by Maharishi Mahesh Yogi (d. 2008). Although he brought TM to the United States as early as the late 1950s, it was only after the Beatles visited him in India in 1968 that his teachings became well known to a Western audience and the popularity of TM took off. TM can best be characterized as a form of "Neo-Hinduism" (Sawyer & Humes, 2023: 1) that basically adopts a monistic ontology which considers the divine (known as *brahman*) a diffuse, amorphous, yet ever-present life force that pervades everything (Rothstein, 2004). Indeed, in TM, "Reality is a Oneness made up of manifest things that arise from their transcendent source in the Being – and since we too, on the level of our physical selves, are some of the things arising from that transcendental Being, we too are not separate from it" (Sawyer & Humes, 2023: 10). According to this typically monistic teaching, the divine resides within each individual and can be accessed by means of meditation techniques (Wallis, 2003). In addition to TM and Westernized forms of Hinduism, many baby boomers became fascinated with the monistic vision contained in Buddhism – or at least its Westernized versions (Altglas, 2014). Thus, many flocked to the Japanese-born Soka Gakkai movement, known in the United States as Nichiren Soshu of America, and in Britain as Nichiren Soshu of the United Kingdom. Now known as Soka Gakkai International (SGI), the movement teaches that all individuals should seek to realize their "Buddha nature" (Métraux, 2013).

What made this ontological shift from religious dualism to monism possible was not only the generational disenchantment with traditional Christianity, but also the increased exposure to imported Asian religious ideas and practices. For at the very moment when Western baby boomers were becoming disillusioned with the Christianity of their parents, they were introduced to a host of gurus and teachers from Asia, who skillfully adapted their exotic teachings to fit Western values and assumptions. In fact, while it remains true that many NRMs owe much to Asia, it would be inaccurate to see them as wholly foreign to the West, because metaphysical monism also had a long history in Europe, dating back to at least the Renaissance (Hanegraaff, 1996). This "Eastern" tradition *within* the West, as Campbell calls it (2007), blossomed in nineteenth-century Europe and America in the form of movements such as Spiritualism, Mesmerism, Transcendentalism, New Thought, and Theosophy (see Fuller, 2001; Bender, 2010; Schmidt, 2012). These sundry movements typically combined Asian teachings and practices with Romantic sensibilities and ideals.

At the other end of the spectrum, we find monisms which are indebted to the Western esoteric tradition – a tradition that has been rejected, stigmatized, and marginalized by Christianity (e.g., Barkun, 2006). Most notable are Pagan movements like Wicca or the Church of All Worlds, which often romanticize an imagined premodern past wherein the divine, the natural world, and humanity existed in holistic and enchanted harmony (Luhrmann, 1991 [1989]; Hanegraaff, 1996; Adler, 1997[1986]).

While the 1960s not only sparked interest in (typically Westernized) "Eastern" religion and "Western" forms of monism (e.g., esotericism, Paganism), they also set off a Christian revival, with nontraditional forms of Christianity popping up left and right. The most prominent of these were the Charismatic and Pentecostal movements, which have since spread across the globe (D. Martin, 2002). While Pentecostal and Charismatic Christians do not reject the idea of a God who is radically transcendent, Charismatic ontology is nevertheless remarkably monistic (Hunt, Hamilton, & Walter, 1997; Poloma, 2003; Campbell, 2007). As anthropologist Simon Coleman (2000: 235) explains, "These Christians worship a God who is both within the self and a permanently moving force on the earth as a whole." So, while Charismatics retain the characteristically Christian notion of a personal deity, they combine this with a holistic conception of God's relationship to humans, which promises each and every individual ready access to God's presence and power in this world. The result is many Christian-inspired NRMs bearing ideological resemblances to Asian imports. For example, Barker observes in her 1984 study of the Unification Church that although the movement retained certain traditional dualisms, it simultaneously embraced the counterculture's holism, treating as sacred ideals of harmony, wholeness and, of course, unity. Like other NRMs, then, the Unification Church reflected a syncretism of Western and Eastern religious thought (Wallis, 2003).

## Religious Epistemology

The shift to a more monistic religious ontology brought with it a shift in epistemology. Following the ideal-typological analysis of Hanegraaff (1996), there have existed three competing epistemologies within the Western tradition: *reason*, *faith*, and *gnosis*. The Middle Ages were a period of religious faith, when doctrine-based epistemologies prevailed. The Enlightenment, then, marked a period when reason rose to prominence, as modern science and rationality were heralded as essential tools in the emancipation of humankind. Finally, according to Hanegraaff, gnostic epistemologies, which ground claims to truth in personal experience, feeling, and intuition, have since the Renaissance been marginalized in the West.

The counterculture and the NRMs it fostered foregrounded precisely such "gnosis," underscoring their preoccupation with personal experience rather than modern science and technology (reason) or traditional religion (faith). As Robert Wuthnow (2003: 104) puts it, "the freedom that triumphed in the 1960s was freedom to feel one's own feelings and to experience one's own sensibilities." We see this clearly in the NRMs of the era. Donald Stone (1976: 95) writes about his study of the Human Potential Movement, which began as an academic enterprise based on the psychology of Carl Gustav Jung (1875–1961) and other post-Freudian psychologists, but soon morphed into a potent site of spiritual seeking: "Whether participants seek cosmic bliss or the pleasure of the moment, they all have in common the quest for direct experience through an expanded consciousness or awareness." Likewise, in her study of Pentecostals and Charismatics ("P/C"), sociologist Margaret Poloma (2003: 23) observes that both "tend to be anticreedal, believing that 'knowing' comes from a right relationship with God," concluding that "the P/C worldview is experientially centered." It is indeed hardly surprising that most NRMs endorse an experiential epistemology, because if the ontology of the divine is conceived monistically as an omnipresent life force or energy, it follows logically that subjective experience will be considered the medium through which one receives divine guidance or insight. A renewed appreciation for feelings and experience thus became a hallmark of the 1960s, with the newly emerging NRMs being first of all "religions of experience" (Dawson, 1998: 138).

At first glance, some might presume that, due to this gnostic epistemology, NRMs would be averse to science. The truth is, however, more complicated than this, because NRM members commonly viewed their own specific religious or spiritual beliefs as perfectly compatible with science. An example is Transcendental Meditation. Meditation is often understood as a spiritual practice promising "a direct, inner, mystical experience of the Self," so that "when that experience becomes permanent . . . the meditator reaches a state of spiritual enlightenment" (Sawyer & Humes, 2023: 8). But it is simultaneously presented as a secular, scientifically sound technique to reduce stress and improve health – even by its founder Maharishi Mahesh Yogi (25). TM is moreover sometimes seen as potentially proving the claims of (quantum) physics by facilitating experiences of "transcendental consciousness" (Rothstein, 2004). Another example is Scientology claiming that all of its religious assertions can be verified through science and experimentation (Rothstein, 2004). In fact, L. Ron Hubbard (1911–1986), who founded the Church of Scientology in California in 1956, presented its self-improvement program Dianetics as grounded in science. He even (unsuccessfully) sought legitimation for these claims by the American Medical Association and the American Psychological Association (Bigliardi, 2023: 6). Overall, then, many NRMs have stressed that spiritual searching, much like scientific inquiry, relies on empirical observation – the only difference being that it demands sensitizing oneself to one's own feelings, bodily sensations, and inner thoughts. In some cases, the claim is even made that this experiential form of empirical investigation is epistemically superior because it captures the underlying holistic reality that remains invisible in the reductionistic-dualistic approach of modern science (Hanegraaff, 1996). Their emphasis on experience also explains why these NRMs place so much emphasis on concrete practices like chanting, meditating, praying, or different forms of bodywork, such as yoga, tantra, Reichian therapies, or breathing exercises. After all, these are activities that aim to induce subjective experiences, altered states, ecstatic emotions, and out-of-the-ordinary feelings that allegedly provide direct access to the divine. Successful recruitment of new followers depends heavily upon this promise of accessing deep, spiritual experience through techniques. Indeed, instead of believing claims of NRMs – made by their leaders and written in foundational texts – one is encouraged to *experience the truth* by just trying out some of these practices. In NRMs varying from Christian evangelical movements to New Age, Lyon argues: "Belief is demoted, experience promoted" (2000: 94). At the same time, such subjective spiritual experiences are often the starting point of socialization – or rather, the slow, gradual "interpretive drift" in which experience and cognitions develop in tandem so that beliefs, postulated by NRMs, become more plausible (Luhrmann, 1991 [1989]).

Their emphasis on experience also helps clarify why NRMs adopted the organizational forms and structures of authority they did. This is because an experiential epistemology tends to give life to one of two organizational dynamics. At one extreme, it may lead to what Campbell (2002[1972]) has dubbed a "cultic milieu," defined by what he elsewhere (Campbell, 2007: 134) calls "epistemological individualism" – each individual having "his or her own version of the truth." Such a diffuse milieu, which facilitates the adoption of ideas, practices, and products in accordance with one's present whims and fancies, is a logical outcome of the primacy of experience. This is because, as Hammer (2001: 331) explains, "There's no need to believe in any particular doctrine, nor is one obliged to trust in their antiquity or their scientific basis. The ultimate litmus test is whether you can experience their veracity for yourself." This first scenario is indeed an apt description of the New Age and Human Potential movements, both of which place a premium on allowing individuals to find and tread their own unique "spiritual path" (Campbell, 2007: 130) through experience. Within the holistic New Age milieu, writes Heelas (1996: 23), "The 'individual' serves as his or her own source of guidance," which indeed rules out stable and enduring organizational forms.

At the other extreme, however, an experiential epistemology can also underpin more hierarchical and structured organizational forms. This is the case if these forms have their roots in what Max Weber (1978 [1921/22]) referred to as "charismatic" authority, as opposed to its traditional and rational counterparts. For if an NRM is led by a charismatic leader, experience remains the authoritative source of spiritual truth, even though here the leader's experiences and intuitions are privileged over those of rank-and-file members (Hammer, 2004). Charismatic churches are a good example. Their stability rests upon the ability of the pastor to temper and rein in the spiritual intuitions of their members, and to privilege their own experiences and insights above those of others. In that sense, David Martin (2002: 13) writes, "Pentecostalism invites an antinomian anarchy which can only be kept from dissolving the assembly in confusion by exercise of pastoral oversight."

Interestingly, the evolution of the Church of Scientology reflects a gradual shift from a relatively antinomian organizational form, premised on an egalitarian epistemological individualism, to a deeply hierarchical and authoritarian organizational form, rooted in a privileging of the supposedly divine revelations of L. Ron Hubbard. As Wallis (1975) outlines, as Scientology grew in stature and membership, there was increased pressure on members to adhere to official doctrine. This enforced conformity was justified on the grounds that these interpretations were rooted in the direct experiences of the leader. Of course, Scientology is far from alone in this. Many, if not most, NRMs exhibit a similar dynamic – which is why they have long been considered controversial. The commonplace fears of NRMs brainwashing their adherents emerge out of the fact that some followers have become so enamored with their leader that they are willing to exploit themselves, harm others, and even commit crimes for the leader. While such extremism is by no means typical, it is a predictable and understandable outcome of an experiential epistemology. What takes place in such instances is that the leader's experiences and intuitions have been imbued with the highest epistemic authority, such that they have come to define and delimit reality for their followers.

## Religious Soteriology

Due to their entanglement with the Romantic worldview the vast majority of NRMs hold that self-realization is imperative: one needs to express the authentic, inner or deeper self and become "who one really is." This is the highest good, the telos of human life. Indeed, conceiving of life in a modern society as utterly alienating, disenchanted, and meaningless, NRMs turn the Romantic ethic of self-expression and self-realization into a spiritual quest for salvation.

We see this, for instance, in the Human Potential Movement – itself a nebulous collection of groups and activities associated with the more academic wing of the counterculture – and its offshoots. One of the most prominent among the latter was Erhard Seminars Training (est), which ran 60-hour training sessions for individuals seeking self-expression, self-improvement, and self-actualization. Other examples include the Inner Peace Movement, founded in 1964 by Francisco Coll (d. 1999), and Insight, both of which boasted effective methods for achieving spiritual and psychological growth. Like many other post-psychoanalytic schools of therapy, these groups subscribed to the notion that the goal of therapeutic programs is to enable an individual to realize their authentic self or, as psychotherapist Carl Rogers (1961: 169) puts it, "to be that self which one truly is." Indeed, the ideal of self-realization as a form of salvation lies at the core of talk of "human potential" (Hanegraaff, 1996). In line with the Romanticist worldview, this spiritual quest to contact a deeper, authentic, or spiritual self lying underneath the different roles we play, is intimately connected with a critique of modern society. Like other NRMs, the Human Potential Movement asserted that individuals could only "transcend the oppressiveness of culture by transforming themselves" (Stone, 1976: 93). In this way, although practitioners of est, the Inner Peace Movement, and Insight may have seemed selfishly committed to their own betterment, the philosophy of these movements made no distinction between self-transformation and world-transformation. On the contrary, it was a central tenet that the source of world betterment is self-improvement on a mass scale. This is equally true of the New Age movement. As Hanegraaff (1996: 281) explains, according to New Age religion, "the supreme moral task is not to do what is good and avoid evil, but, rather, to develop one's inner potential."

The language to describe this source of salvation – the "inner self" – differs between NRMs and is framed through various traditions. It may be called the higher self (derived from Theosophy), divine spark (the gnostic tradition), inner Buddha (Buddhism), inner child (humanistic psychology), or even simply the soul (Christianity). Salvation lies in a variety of spiritual practices that allegedly unlock human potential and that may be either individually or collectively performed. The latter is the case in Paganism where the "magical" or "divine" self may be liberated through collective rituals, procedures, and performances: "Look within yourself; everything for which you are searching is there; Know thou art Goddess / know thou art God" (Berger, 1999: 33). Pagans assume that once the "magical self" has been awakened, one leaves the profane world and enters the sacred world of nature, where everything is possible and holistically interconnected.

The soteriological focus on finding and expressing the inner self is not limited to world-affirming NRMs like the Human Potential Movement, the Bhagwan Movement (Osho), or more recent New Age currents, but is also central to more world-rejecting NRMs. The Unification Church, for instance, requires members to center their lives around God, conforming to the rules and regulations of the church and to evangelize in order to save humanity. However, here too, the prescription is methodologically individualistic. As Barker observes about Unification theology,

> To change the world it is men's hearts, not the system, which must be changed. Blame is never allocated to structures. It is man's motives which should be changed to lead a God-centered life. Each individual should strive to live in uniting and complementary give-and-take relationships both at the horizontal level (as between brothers) and at the vertical level (as between man and God, or parent and child). (Barker, 1978: 84)

We also find a marked Romantic expressivism in the Charismatic Christian movements. As D. Martin (2002: 169) puts it, "Pentecostalism ... is about finding your voice." What he means by this is that, although Pentecostals and Charismatics speak often about obeying God's will, what they mean by this is God's will as it manifests as the "voice within." Much like members of the Human Potential and New Age movements, or Paganism, Charismatic Christians hold that achieving salvation amounts to becoming who they truly are – which is who God intended them to be. And vice versa: finding one's true self is associated with finding God. Thus, we might say this conception of salvation presupposes an ideal of positive freedom, which Harold Bloom (1992: 26) refers to as a "purely inner freedom." Moreover, achieving this involves identifying and overcoming the internal barriers that impede recovery of the authentic and divine core that defines one's true identity. D. Martin (2002: 169) therefore concludes that Charismatic Christianity amounts to "an adaptable form of heart-work and spiritual self-exploration."

According to Wallis (2003), what distinguishes est, the Inner Peace Movement, Insight, New Age, and certain forms of Pentecostalism from other NRMs, is their world-affirming and/or world-accommodating character – meaning, their embrace of modern society and its sociocultural norms. In some respects this is accurate. As we demonstrate in the following section, particularly contemporary "spiritual" New Age groups often willingly embrace the institutions of modern capitalism and apply spiritual techniques to achieve worldly ends (see Heelas, 1999). However, the distinctions between world-affirming, world-accommodating, and world-rejecting can also mislead, for they tend to obscure the underlying cultural similarities. A case in point is that they share the soteriology of self-expression, personal growth, or self-realization. Most scholars of NRMs agree, for instance, that one of the most prominent world-rejecting movements has been the International Society for Krishna Consciousness. No doubt, the Hare Krishnas stand out in light of the strict lifestyle, diet, and dress code they follow. Because of ISKCON's asceticism and apparent exoticism, observers have tended to stress its differences from more world-affirming movements of the New Age variety. Nevertheless, the commitments of Hare Krishnas, too, are ultimately grounded in a desire for self-realization as salvation. As Rochford (2007: 10–11) explains, the spokesperson of ISKCON, Caitanya, "preached that all people, regardless of their caste or position in life, could gain self-realization by serving Krishna... Central to this process of self-realization is chanting the Hare Krishna mantra."

In short, even the most world-rejecting NRMs typically espouse the same religious soteriology as the most world-affirming and world-accommodating ones.

The opposite applies as well. Despite the fact that the Human Potential and New Age adepts are accommodationist in crucial respects – nowadays affirming rather than rejecting free-market capitalism and private property – it would be wrong to see them as entirely uncritical of mainstream society. For Romantic expressivism always contains within itself a strident critique of society, which frames conformism to social norms and conventions as major impediments to the pursuit of self-realization. As Bellah (1976) argued, most NRMs in the 1960s already shared a rejection of utilitarian individualism which holds that the goal of life is to maximize self-interest. Many also shared with the social and political movements of the era a rejection of traditional racial, gender, sex, and lifestyle norms and conventions, which countercultural baby boomers saw as stifling and repressive (see Watts, 2022). Rather than distinguishing world-rejecting, world-affirming, or world-accommodating NRMs, it therefore makes more sense to emphasize that their religious soteriologies of seeking, finding, and expressing the real self entail a countercultural stance that is either implicitly or explicitly grounded in a Romantic critique of modernity.

## NRMs: Theodical Unity in Diversity

Although NRMs exhibit a manifest diversity in their doctrines, practices, and organizational forms, they nevertheless share an underlying cultural logic that consists of three interrelated dimensions: (1) a distinctive religious ontology that replaces dualism with a monistic-holistic perspective on nature; (2) an epistemology that places emphasis, not on belief or faith but on subjective experience as a path to truth; and (3) a soteriology which sees self-realization as the sole route to the ultimate goal of salvation. Many of the Romantic NRMs are organized around fresh interpretations of Asian religions, for example, Hare Krishna, TM, or the Rajneesh movement, while others build on Western Pagan currents, such as Wicca, revisiting or re-inventing traditions and worldviews featuring animism, polytheism, and magic. Notwithstanding this diversity, these NRMs share a cultural logic that is informed by the spirit of Romanticism. This even applies to those that build on Western Christianity, such as the Unification Church or Pentecostal movements. Just like their non-Christian counterparts, these movements have a "common emphasis on intense, even ecstatic, emotional experience" through spiritual, self-oriented practices, and their aim is similar: "to achieve wholeness" (Campbell, 2006: 347).

Many studies have completely overlooked this cultural unity underlying NRMs. Our cultural-sociological approach helps to make clear that the collective emergence of NRMs in the 1960s was neither coincidental nor a temporary historical blip. It was grounded in the widespread dissatisfaction among baby boomers with long-standing (Christian) dogmas, "churched" religion, and alienating social systems and, based on this, their active reconstruction of religion and culture in and through NRMs. More than anything else, NRMs between the 1950s and 1970s were laboratories of cultural resistance, social experimentation, and religious innovation. In these NRMs' "new" theodicies of ultimate meaning – underpinned by Romantic ontologies, epistemologies and soteriologies – were actively constructed and established. It is the "new" Romanticism of NRMs that, in turn, informed widespread societal antagonism during this turbulent period. From a historical-sociological perspective, the question remains how stable and persistent such cultural-religious innovations have proven to be over the last decades. In NRM studies, this question is often raised as, "When do New Religions stop being new?" or relatedly, "How sustainable are New Religious Movements over time?" (e.g., Barker, 2004). Romantic NRMs are, after all, nontraditional by nature: during the period of the counterculture they were generally built on charismatic leadership emphasizing subjective experience, such that "few guarantees of survival existed." Moreover, members were first-generation converts, making intergenerational transmission from parents to children unlikely. On top of this, many NRM memberships already turned out to be unstable and volatile during the 1960s and 1970s, with romantic-religious seekers pursuing better, higher, and deeper spiritual experiences often switching their allegiances from one NRM to another—a dynamic encouraged by the increasingly competitive "market of ultimate significance" (Luckmann, 1967: 99).

So what happens when New (Romantic) Religions stop being new? Taking a historical-sociological approach, we will argue in the next two sections that the ideologies and practices of NRMs persisted over the last decades, but that their social form has changed. Instead of their typical lack of "alignment" with the "dominant culture," their countercultural protest against "the structure and interests of dominant institutions" (Bromley, 2004: 92), and their social positioning on "the fringes of society" (Melton, 2004: 73), NRM ideologies and practices have become part and parcel of dominant institutional domains like work, health, media, games, and technology.

## 3 Institutionalization

Already in 1976, the sociologist Daniel Bell (1976: 143) reflected critically on the counterculture and its new religions, stating that "the main tendency of that ideology – though it appeared in the guise of an attack on the 'technocratic society' – was an attack on reason itself." From TM, to the Rajneesh movement, to Wicca, and the New Age Movement to the neo-Reichian movements or the Church of Satan – Bell depicted NRMs as a danger to modern institutions because of their emphasis on "spontaneity, on orgiastic release, on sensory communication, on Eastern mysticism and ritual" (Bell, 1976: 140). Indeed, it was the typically Romantic worldview, the ontology of monism, epistemology of experience, and soteriological focus on unlimited emotional self-expression, that provoked moral concern at that time, particularly among older generations adhering to established traditions.

The tensions between the countercultural, Romantic NRMs, and mainstream social institutions have, however, increasingly dissolved over the past fifty years (Watts, 2022). Many NRMs became more world-accommodating or world-affirming. And vice versa: the stigmatization of NRMs and the labeling of their members as deviant, irrational, or even dangerous have dramatically decreased. Examples abound: spiritual practices like meditation or yoga are hardly confined to self-enclosed NRMs or countercultural communities anymore; there's no more need to "drop out" in an Indian Ashram, follow Bhagwan Shree Rajneesh (Osho) or join the TM-movement if one wants to "tune in" to meditation or experience spirituality. NRMs have typically come to cater pragmatically to large and diverse audiences in variegated social contexts (e.g., Jain, 2014).

We will analyze this softening of the boundaries between NRMs and the societal mainstream in this section by using the New Age movement as a paradigmatic example. Like many other NRMs, the New Age movement was originally countercultural and deviant from a societal view. As a "millenarian" movement, it originated in otherworldly UFO cults, Theosophical movements, and millenarian religions in the 1950s and 1960s that predicted the apocalypse and various forms of salvation (e.g., Hanegraaff, 1996; Sutcliffe, 2003). Based on a detailed historical analysis, Sutcliffe demonstrates that the New Age movement evolved over the last decades from an otherworldly millenarian movement – considering "the New Age" as a postapocalyptic future state for an elect group of spiritual people – to an open, humanist quest for connectedness, spiritual experience, and "self-realization in the here-and-now" (2003: 5). A New Age movement in opposition to the established order thus made way for New Age as an umbrella term for a heterogeneous collection of "new," Romantic forms of spirituality that became widespread in the 1980s (Hanegraaff, 1996) and that has since then been rapidly "mainstreaming" (Løøv, 2024: 20). What distinguishes contemporary New Age from most "old-style" NRMs is not just its characteristic organization as an open network (York, 1995) but its Theosophy-informed "perennial" ideology, according to which *all religious traditions are valid* because they all trace back to the same spiritual source (e.g., Hanegraaff, 1996; Heelas, 1996; Possamai, 2005). In the words of a Dutch New Age teacher who is typically "working with" traditions from Hinduism, shamanism, Kabbalah and even various forms of Christianity in his courses: "for me, all religions are manifestations of the divine. If you look beyond the surface, all religions tell the same story" (Aupers & Houtman, 2006: 203).

This, then, is the primary difference between New Age and typical "old-style" NRMs like the Rajneesh movement, ISKCON, Scientology, or Pentecostalism which are all grounded in well-defined traditions, doctrines, and rituals (Sutcliffe, 2003: 198). New Age "perennialism" actually encourages people to draw on multiple religions, not least other NRMs, which results in all sorts of combinations and hybrid mixtures that aim for the same Romantic-religious goals: holistic connectedness, experiences of spiritual truth, and personal growth. This perennialist, inclusivist, and "detraditionalized" character of New Age (Heelas, 1996) accounts for much of its accessibility to a liberal audience and hence much of its popularity and success. At the beginning of the twenty-first century, Sutcliffe and Bowman (2000: 11) even observed in this respect that "contrary to predictions that New Age would go mainstream, now it's as if the mainstream is going New Age." As we will see in this section, New Age thus exemplifies how the Romantic religious logic of the NRMs has increasingly invaded mainstream society, not least the domains of health care and business.

## From Alternative to Complementary Health Care

One of the major ways in which NRMs have transformed the institutional fabric of the West is through their influence on health care. The process is an outcome of the alternative health care paradigm that developed in spiritual circles in the 1960s counterculture, most notably in the San Francisco Bay Area.

Alternative ideas about health and healing are indeed key issues in New Age literature, courses and practices and they "undoubtedly [represent] one of the most visible aspects of the New Age Movement" (Hanegraaff, 1996: 42). These ideas provide answers to questions like "What is health?" "What is (the cause of) illness?" and "How can humans be 'healed'?" which differ significantly from those given by medical science and modern health care. The principal tenet is that modern society produces physical, psychological, and spiritual health problems that modern health care not only cannot cure, but in fact may be the cause of. From the 1960s onwards the paradigm has therefore critically "challenged the bureaucratic, high-tech and iatrogenic aspects of conventional medicine or what medical anthropologists generally refer to as biomedicine" (Baer, 2004: 1).

The healing process is here seen as rooted in a monistic or holistic ontology that understands nature as a restorative power and human beings as capable of curing themselves (e.g., Hanegraaff, 1996; Campbell, 2007). The logic of holistic health in New Age thought does not so much target Christian religious dualism, but the mind-body dualism associated with Enlightenment philosopher René Descartes (1596–1650) that is firmly institutionalized in modern health care. Modern health specialists, it is argued, approach patients as machine-like entities by treating the body, mind, and spirit as isolated and separate. Hence, they require separate professional disciplines and specializations to treat human illness. On the one hand, doctors, surgeons, and pharmacists treat physical illness without considering the mind, emotions, and personal or traumatic experiences as possible causes of physical health issues. In doing so, they allegedly treat symptoms rather than real problems. Psychologists and psychiatrists, on the other hand, analyze the human mind and emotions without taking notice of their fundamental embeddedness in the body. The spiritual dimension, which forges a connection between body and mind and which is taken to be pivotal to what it means to be human in the first place, is thus neglected in both instances. The New Age Movement, but also the related Human Potential Movement, Asian healing groups, and Pagan movements like Wicca, all critique the secular-scientific paradigm for slandering this crucial dimension under the banners of irrationality, superstition, and illusion. They replace the modern dualism that is held responsible for this with a holistic perspective that connects body, mind, and a spiritual life force or energy. Emphasizing the "interconnectedness of all things in the universe" (Løøv, 2024: 33), the holistic approach to health thus differs dramatically from that of conventional modern Western medicine:

> It is ... radically different from the traditional Western model, which typically envisages illness and disease as caused by natural forces that invade or attack the body either from within (such as cancer) or without (as in the case

> of germs and viruses). In either case these have to be countered, that is, beaten off or overcome in some way, through skilled human intervention. This may be by means of drugs, in particular antibiotics, or through the use of vaccines, surgical intervention, or such techniques as chemotherapy. In all cases scientific knowledge and technological skill combine to produce the "weapons" needed in this "war" against "a natural enemy." The [holistic] model could not be more different. Here nature is regarded as the cure rather than as the source of disease, the assumption being that if an individual is ill, then this will be because he or she is not properly "adjusted" to the natural flow of energies that exist within and around him or her. (Campbell, 2007: 102–3)

The dissemination of ideas about holistic healing has popularized a range of therapies that rely on natural remedies – herbs, oils, crystals, sound, light, color – that build on patients' own natural abilities, and that use "non-invasive, hands-on manipulative techniques" (Campbell, 2007: 103). Chiropractic, acupuncture, homeopathy, aromatherapy, Reiki, yoga, tai chi, meditation, Ayurvedic massage, and related therapies stand out as some of the best-known examples. What they have in common is not just that they are based on the Romantic understanding of humans as naturally whole beings, but also on the premise that (human) nature needs to be protected against invasions from the realm of the non-natural, the artificial, the human-made, and the technological. Recovery from disease and acquisition of immunity are seen as natural processes that cannot, and should not, be technologically short-circuited. In the long run, chemical drugs and vaccines are conceived as doing more harm than good, as they ultimately damage the human body's self-healing potential. Hardly surprising, then, this type of Romantic New Age spirituality is a strong predictor of vaccine skepticism and low faith in science alike (Rutjens & van der Lee, 2020; Rutjens et al., 2022; Rutjens, Zarzeczna, & van der Lee 2022). Consequently, during the COVID-19 pandemic in 2020 and 2021 some spiritual practitioners opposed state-led vaccination campaigns (Houtman & Aupers, 2024).

It is no surprise that holistic ideas about health and healing evoked hostility and accusations of quackery from the public and the medical establishment. And yet it has been popularized and normalized over the last decades. Although holistic health continues to meet with scientific skepticism, and its practitioners are sometimes still called "witch doctors" (Brown, 2024) – particularly in extreme cases when patients are advised to reject conventional medical treatments altogether – much of the public resistance to medical alternatives has withered away since the 1990s. Part of the explanation is that self-enclosed NRMs that were freely experimenting with alternative ideas and healing methods have made way for a broad public interest in what is now known as Complementary and Alternative Medicine (CAM). To give an indication: about one-third of the adult population in the United States used some form of CAM between 2002 and 2012, with a significant increase across this period. Particularly holistic practices like yoga, tai chi, and qi gong became more popular, increasing from 5.8 percent in 2002 to 6.7 percent in 2007 and 10.1 percent in 2012 (Clarke et al., 2015). In Europe, over the course of the year 2018, no less than 25 percent of the population used at least one form of CAM – such as manual therapies, alternative medical systems, traditional Asian medical systems, and mind–body therapy.

These data demonstrate a mainstreaming of CAM and its Romantic worldview, but at the same time they show the increased instrumentalization of its use. CAM treatments have been pragmatically integrated into mainstream health care institutions alongside modern biomedicine (Fisher & Ward, 1994; Winnick, 2005). So while initially developed and applied in countercultural NRMs as an alternative to mainstream health care, CAM is now generally used *as a supplement* to modern medical and/or psychological therapies. Holistic health has as such become less and less of an alternative to conventional medicine, having instead evolved into what is nowadays called "integrative" medicine. Given the absence of credible scientific evidence for either the efficacy of holistic healing or its metaphysical underpinnings, this integration of biomedicine and complementary holistic healing is quite remarkable (Brown, 2024). It appears to be a response to public discontents about the impersonal character of modern health care and concerns about its side effects. Among motivations to engage in CAM, we typically find "a preference for natural care instead of biomedical medicine, a desire for more personalized and holistic care, dissatisfaction with biomedicine and dissatisfaction with the doctor–patient relationship" (Kemppainen et al., 2018: 449). The increased clinical significance of holistic health has coincided with processes of professionalization, as exemplified by the establishment of a range of peer-reviewed and scientifically recognized journals devoted to the study of CAM (e.g., *Journal of Integrative and Complementary Medicine*, since 1994; *Journal of Alternative and Complementary Medicine*, since 1995; *Alternative Medicine Review*, since 1996; *BMC Complementary Medicine and Therapies*, since 2001; and *Journal of Traditional and Complementary Medicine*, since 2011).

The increased reliance on holistic health is part and parcel of a more general "re-habilitation of nature" that has occurred since the 1970s (Campbell, 2007). In the wake of concerns about worldwide environmental issues, animal rights, and a Romantic celebration of nature, it is indeed hardly surprising that the appeal of holistic health has increased. Campbell (2007: 97) goes as far as to argue that this turn to nature has resulted in "a revolution in mental therapy," in which it is widely assumed that "health and wholeness are natural conditions and that illness is something created by humans themselves."

While biomedicine and holistic healing have thus become increasingly integrated, it would be incorrect to believe that conflicts between the two paradigms of health and healthcare have disappeared (Barrett et al., 2003) or that their differences no longer give rise to protest and criticism. Advocates of the biomedical model can still be found lamenting that patients are being misled, and this scientific skepticism prompts calls to empirically assess the actual efficacy of holistic therapies by using double-blind randomized control trials – considered the gold standard in scientific circles due to their ability to effectively cancel out so-called placebo effects. However, given that such controlled experiments are informed by the very dualism and reductionism that advocates of holistic health reject, the debate over the validity of CAM goes on. Academically trained Dutch general practitioners who double as holistic healers dismiss the notion that modern biomedicine can actually cure their patients (Raaphorst & Houtman, 2016). They use biomedicine pragmatically to prevent their patients from dying, to be sure, but do nonetheless sharply distinguish between death prevention and health care, the latter conceived holistically. For these doctors, then, seeking refuge in biomedicine entails a necessary, albeit unfortunate, response to long years of health neglect, including that of nonphysical (spiritual) problems that could and should have been treated holistically much earlier on (Raaphorst & Houtman, 2016). Debates and disagreements about the validity, utility, and shortcomings of holistic health and biomedicine still linger, in short, even though visible conflicts appear to be increasingly rare – with the exception of the widespread opposition to COVID-19 vaccines. Meanwhile, the popularity of holistic healthcare and spiritual healing continues to grow.

## Spirituality in Business

Another development that exemplifies the mainstreaming of the Romantic-religious logic of NRMs, particularly in the form of New Age ideas and practices, is its integration into the world of work (Watts & Houtman, 2022). In the 1960s and 1970s, the Romantic counterculture and the NRMs formed in its bosom, powered trenchant critiques of modern capitalism, dismissing it as alienating, dehumanizing, and disenchanting. Things have changed considerably. Since the 1980s, many adherents of the New Age movement have ceased to think of work and life, profit and self-expression, and capitalism and spirituality as irreconcilable. Quite the contrary. According to Paul Heelas (1996), the aim became increasingly to overcome work-life "schizophrenia" and to shift to more world-affirming approaches. The process is evident in the increasing

## New Religious Movements and the Romantic Spirit of Modernity 31

integration of various forms of New Age spirituality and business. Pointing out the business world's interest in and adoption of New Age ideas, Human Potential courses, and Asian practices such as Zen meditation and hatha yoga, Heelas (1996: 30) observes: "Inner spirituality is here utilized as a means to experiencing the best of the outer world, rather than being intrinsically valued. Downplaying, even ignoring the role played by detachment, the emphasis is now on empowerment and prosperity."

The first examples of "New Age capitalism" or the "prosperity wing" of the New Age movement, as Heelas (1996) calls it, emerged in the 1970s in the United States and have since spread across the globe. Perhaps the most influential example is Erhard Seminars Training (est). Its founder Werner Erhard (b. 1935) was an active member of the Church of Scientology, but also offered spiritual seminars based on a mixture of gestalt therapy, psychosynthesis, Zen meditation, and management training. Unlike most countercultural gurus, he encouraged participants to use spiritual insights to function better in private life and at work alike. Under the motto "Whatever the world is doing, go do that," est exemplifies a new approach combining the "best of both worlds" – the spiritual world of holism (valuing inner spirituality, self-expression) and business life (work, efficiency, and personal success).

According to the sociologist Steven Tipton (1982), this approach became successful in the 1970s for two related reasons. On the one hand, countercultural members of NRMs became disappointed and disenchanted with the revolutionary ideals, promises, and prophecies of a coming New Age of Aquarius. This led the emphasis in the New Age milieu to shift from social transformation to personal spiritual growth. On the other hand, having had their formative years in the 1960s and cherishing self-expression as the highest value, many felt increasingly stifled in their nine-to-five routines, imprisoned in Weber's (2005 [1904/5]) "iron cage" of modern working life. Reporting on the "efforts of soul-seeking, spirituality, sensual re-enchantments and self-expressivism" among this cohort at the dawn of the twenty-first century, Casey (2004: 72, 76) writes: "Their activities are responses to experienced lackings in overly rationalized, instrumentalized and dispirited bureaucratic organizations and industrially disciplined workplaces." Indeed, as self-expression and spirituality became the core ideals for private life in the wake of the 1960s, many workers – especially among the professional-managerial class – began to yearn for an integration of those ideals in their professional lives, too. Est was one of the first and one of the most popular seminars that tried to combine these worlds:

> EST defines what is intrinsically valuable in self-expressive categories consonant with counter-cultural ideals. Then it uses these personally fulfilling

> and expressive ends to justify the routine work and goal achievement of mainstream public life. "Work hard and achieve your goals in order to feel alive and natural," EST advises in effect. This formula justifies 1960s youth dropping back into middle-class economic and social life. And it motivates them to lead this life effectively, with an eye to inner satisfaction as well as external success. (Tipton, 1982: 281; capitalization as in original)

The goals of "inner satisfaction" and "external success" were, thus, reconciled in est trainings, and this synthesis has become more mainstream ever since. In 1984, Erhard founded Erhard Transformational Technologies, which invited companies to attend its seminars. Other examples from this same period include Lifespring and the Silva Mind Control Method ("Use the power of your mind to increase your sales"). Bhagwan Shree Rajneesh (aka Osho, 1931–1990), who mobilized holistic ontologies to coin the term "materialist spirituality" and to deconstruct the dichotomies of spirituality versus prosperity, work versus detachment, and this-worldliness versus other-worldliness, even offered trainings in "efficiency management."

The mainstreaming of "workplace spirituality" is also captured by the increased popularity of commercial courses and the booming business of self-help literature. In sociological terms, the New Age evolved from an alternative "cult movement" to a commercial "client and audience cult" offering spiritual services (Stark & Bainbridge, 1985: 209). New Age became a broad cultural phenomenon oriented toward people in all layers of society, functions, and professions (Hanegraaff, 1996). This development was initiated from within the spiritual milieu itself, where adherents dropped out of formal, narrowly enclosed NRMs and cults in order to take advantage of an attractive spiritual approach to everyday issues like work and prosperity. Meanwhile, companies, business organizations, and managers co-opted spirituality in the 1980s, considering it valuable, or plainly strategic, to take a more humanistic or spiritual stance. Indeed, management literature formerly emphasizing rational reasoning, strategic thinking, and instrumentality, began to open up to spiritual discourse in the 1980s. Titles like *The I-Ching on Business and Decision-making* (Damian-Knight, 1986), *The Intuitive Manager* (Rowan, 1986), and *Working and Managing in a New Age* (Garland, 1990) demonstrate this shift. Influential management gurus like Tony Robbins and Stephen Covey emerged and destigmatized spirituality, introducing it to a large audience. In bestsellers like *Unlimited Power* (1997 [1989]) and *Awaken the Giant Within: How to Take Immediate Control of Your Mental, Physical and Financial Destiny* (1991), Robbins connected "inner power" with societal status and success. In *The Seven Habits of Highly Effective People: Powerful Lessons in Personal Change* (1992 [1989]) Stephen Covey, a member of the Church of Jesus Christ of Latter-day

Saints, argued for a veritable paradigm shift through an "inside-out approach" in business life by opening up to personal growth and spiritual experience.

In addition to this self-help literature focusing on individual managers, a growing number of management journals such as *People Management*, *Industry Week*, and *Sloan Management Review* started giving explicit attention to the role of spirituality in business organizations. Reviewing this literature, which also took off in the 1980s, we find that the Romantic critique of technocratic thinking is paradoxically co-opted and incorporated to serve the interests of business. The management scholars involved decry narrowly prescribed work roles, functions, and positions in hierarchical organizational structures as dehumanizing, because they alienate people from who they really are – their deeper, inner, or "spiritual selves." Donde Ashmos and Dennis Duchon (2000: 136) correctly observe that the spiritual discourse in the world of business is an attempt to demolish the problematic segregation between the private and the public realm and, in doing so, to re-introduce a sense of personal meaning or "soul" at the workplace: "The spirituality at work movement is about more meaningful work, about connection between the soul and work." In the same vein, based on extensive in-depth interviews and 2,000 surveys in American companies in the 1990s, Mitroff and Denton (1999: 14) conclude that it is pivotal for organizations to integrate spirituality:

> This age calls for a new "spirit of management." For us, the concepts of spirituality and soul are not merely add-on elements of a new philosophy or policy ... No management effort can survive without them. We refuse to accept that whole organizations cannot learn ways to foster soul and spirituality in the workplace. We believe not only that they can, but also that they must.

Even though these arguments are clearly derived from the Romantic counterculture, they are hardly formulated as critiques of the goals and foundations of modern capitalism. Although some refer to the need for a paradigm shift in business life, most calls for holism, authenticity, experience, and self-expression actually respect the neatly defined boundaries of traditional economic and instrumental management thinking. Drawing on the holistic perspective, the argument is simply that there is no conflict between economic striving and spiritual development, so that we are dealing with a win-win situation. Here, happy people are considered efficient people, or as Klein and Izzo (1998: 18) put it, "work is about spirit as much as salary." Intrinsically motivated people guided by "inner spirituality" allegedly experience less stress in their job, and are much more productive, communicative, creative, and competitive, which is profitable for every organization. Starting from this assumption, countless commercial centers and professional trainers have emerged in the United States and Western Europe since the 1990s, offering their spiritual services to companies in order to accommodate Romantic longings for self-realization with capitalist profit seeking.

One of our own studies in the Netherlands (Aupers & Houtman, 2006) shows the goals, worldviews, and practices of this spiritual industry emerging in the 1990s. One of the first and most influential centers was Oibibio, founded in Amsterdam in 1993 by Ronald-Jan Heijn. Oibibio's business department offered training in spiritual management, such as "Team management and the soul" and "Management in astrological perspective," aimed at keeping companies "ready for battle" during times when "dynamic streams of production, services and information increasingly put pressure on organizations and managers." They made the following claim in their flyer: "Our trainers are builders of bridges: they speak the language of business life and pragmatically know how to implant the spiritual philosophy in your organization; they do so in cooperation with your employees" (Aupers & Houtman, 2006: 212). Although Oibibio went bankrupt in the late 1990s, this certainly did not trigger a decline of New Age capitalism in the Netherlands. Instead, its bankruptcy marked the birth of many other, more successful New Age centers, such as Metavisie, Soulstation, Being in Business, and Firmament. Such centers typically describe their services as follows:

> The mission of Being in Business is to build a bridge between organisations and spirituality to make businesses more successful. Success, then, is not primarily defined as making more profit, but also as increasing well-being for you and your employees. Being in Business shapes this spiritual dimension in your organisation by providing services that will increase consciousness, vitality, fun, pleasure and energy. Spirituality is profit. Because profit is nothing more than materialized energy. The more energy your organisation generates, the higher the profit. And spirituality in your organisation is of course much more. (Cited in Aupers & Houtman, 2006: 213)

In the wake of the 1990s, spirituality thus ceased to be incompatible with work, commercial goals, and business life. Corporate as well as governmental organizations – from banks to insurance companies and government ministries – started offering spiritual training to their employees. Examples include Guinness, General Dynamics, Boeing Aerospace, and even the US Army (Heelas, 1996). More recently, Dennis LoRusso (2017: 5) has observed that common managerial sense increasingly dictates that, "business leaders and managers have an obligation to attend to the spiritual needs of their employees." This wisdom has been imbibed by companies as large as Google, Nike, and Salesforce, each of which now carves out "physical spaces where individuals may 'recharge' through relaxation, meditation, or engage in daily prayers" (Gog et al., 2020: 5). Google even established its own mindfulness-based management training program, called *Search Inside Yourself*, which has meanwhile been exported to business schools around the globe.

Naisbitt and Aburdene (1990: 273) refer to a survey of 500 American companies, at least half of which had, at some point, offered "consciousness-raising techniques" to their employees. It is estimated that in the 1990s American companies spent at least $4 billion annually on New Age consultants, accounting for more than 10 percent of the $30 billion spent on company training each year (Swets & Bjork, 1990; Nadesan, 1999). Perhaps the best illustration are offerings of Zen meditation or mindfulness training to employees in companies such as Google, General Mills, Intel, Goldman Sachs, Nike, and AstraZeneca. Even though such in-company trainings and consciousness-raising techniques are for obvious reasons not always explicitly referred to as "spiritual" in such professional contexts, their Romantic religious underpinnings remain in play.

Meditation has been increasingly adapted to a Western context and disconnected from Asian traditions, since its introduction through Helena Blavatsky's Theosophy in the second half of the nineteenth century. Among Beat Poets like Jack Kerouac, Lawrence Ferlinghetti, and Allen Ginsberg – open-minded, spirituality-seeking rebels and forerunners of the counterculture in the 1950s – meditation was still primarily a countercultural practice aimed at detaching from the burdens of everyday life and work routines. Its principal contemporary offshoot, mindfulness, has however become almost completely disconnected from any religious and spiritual roots, and is now presented as a neutral, efficient technique to discipline the self (Cortois, Aupers, & Houtman, 2018). This disconnection from religion explains much of its popularity in business organizations where, as Kucinskas (2018) observes, the "mindful elite" is collectively trained to be productive and stay competitive in the context of contemporary capitalism. In her book *Selling Yoga: From Counter Culture to Pop Culture*, Andrea Jain (2014) takes this analysis a step further, characterizing the common practice of yoga in contemporary business life as "neo-liberal spirituality." She considers in-company yoga training as capitalism's latest trick to control employees, now that hierarchical and authoritarian modes of control have lost their former legitimacy. From a more general stance, spirituality in business life has become part and parcel of what Boltanski and Chiapello (2007) call "the new spirit of capitalism" – an exercise in "soft power" derived from the artistic, creative, and expressivist ethic of the Western counterculture.

Whereas advocates applaud attempts at bringing "the soul back to work," critics point out the logic of capitalism that underlies such initiatives by emphasizing its role as a new, concealed mode of social control (Watts & Houtman, 2022). Even so, it is quite clear that Romantic religion has increasingly found its place in the business world. In short, this development signifies a marked shift from world-rejecting – and even millenarian – forms of New Age spirituality, practiced in enclosed communities that sustain a tension with the outside world, to a more world-affirming stance in which spirituality is mobilized in work and everyday life. And of course, the argument can also be formulated the other way around: spiritual New Age training – from Human Potential courses, yoga, and reiki to mindfulness meditation – have lost much of their former social stigma as deviant, fuzzy, irrational, or dangerous. Much like holistic health, mindfulness has been de-stigmatized and normalized in the twenty-first century. In the next section, we discuss a much neglected cause of this increased social and public significance of Romantic forms of religion: their dissemination in and through movies, television series, and videogames, and their subsequent penetration into the heart of Silicon Valley's high-tech industry.

## 4 Mediatization

Media contents – texts, stories, and narratives – both mirror and shape the culture in which they are produced, such that they "constantly feed into and are themselves fed by the makeup and character of society" (Hodkinson, 2017: 5). Indeed, all media narratives, including those that are presented as fiction, are not only deeply informed by shared cultural values and norms in society; they are also key in social and cultural agenda-setting and priming individuals toward particular beliefs (2017: 5). Guided by this assumption, we demonstrate in this section that the religious logic of NRMs – once contested, demonized, and elevated to crisis proportions in and through mainstream media – is nowadays appropriated and popularized by the culture industry. We document this particularly for the marked presence of the Romantic Pagan movement in movies, television series, and video games.

Like New Age, Paganism is an ideal-typological umbrella term that encompasses religious groups in many flavors and forms, such as Wicca, the Church of All Worlds, occultist groups, and even satanic Paganism. Indeed, Paganism strongly resembles New Age in many respects (York, 1995; Hanegraaff, 1996; Campbell, 2007) since, as Partridge claims, "New Agers and Pagans are drinking from the same conceptual pool" (2004: 79) and they share the same perennialist ideology: pagans typically delve in different historical traditions – from esotericism, Greek mythology, historical accounts of witchcraft to fantasy fiction – in order to construct their "personal" pagan worldview. The striking difference with New Age, however, is that Paganism is a more nature-based, animistic, and polytheistic religion that is distinctly "romanticizing the premodern" (Partridge, 2004: 77). Whereas New Age tends to emphasize *spirit over matter*, Pagans radically situate *spirit in matter* (Campbell, 2007: 127). The natural environment, the animal world, clouds, trees, and rocks are understood as belonging to a vital and sentient environment. Pagans worship various gods and goddesses, while magical practices, rituals, and spells stand out as most important in the Pagan milieu. As one of Pagan practitioner Margot Adler's respondents says: "It's a religion of ritual rather than theology. The ritual is first, the myth is second" (Adler, 1986: 170). Through magical rituals in nature Pagans seek to invoke and experience the divine "power-from-within" (York, 1995: 107) and to bring about a general re-enchantment of the world. As Hanegraaff notes, "neopagan magic ... functions as a means of invoking and reaffirming mystery in a world that seems to have lost it" (1996: 84).

This Paganism, we demonstrate next, has become abundantly mediatized over the last decades, that is, is massively represented in and disseminated through the narratives of films, TV series, and digital games. Processes of digitization have not only launched Paganism into interactive game worlds, but have even given rise to NRMs formed around technologies such as virtual reality, artificial intelligence, and biotech.

## Occulture in Fiction, Film, and Television

In the 1960s and 1970s, NRMs were still chiefly considered deviant and sometimes even dangerous. Their increased popularity among young people in the 1960s triggered what can be called a wave of "moral panic" (Cohen, 1972). Worried parents, priests, politicians, and groups like the anticult movement considered NRMs the ultimate symbol of evil – a "folk devil" and scapegoat blamed for the decline of established Christianity and common decency. Mass media played a vital role in stirring this moral panic and intensifying tensions between NRMs and the societal mainstream. News media reported on NRMs in a highly sensationalistic fashion by selecting the most extreme examples and relying on *pars pro toto* stigmatization, stereotypes, exaggeration, and distortion (Richardson & Introvigne, 2007). Fictional books and movies at the time often portrayed NRMs and alternative religious ideas as evil Others. Movies exhibited a veritable "Satanic scare" and generated a more general fear of esotericism, Paganism, and occultism by juxtaposing "good" Christianity with "bad" Pagan religion or imagery. Their narratives dramatically framed the latter as a horrifying threat to Western society in general, and to vulnerable, pure, innocent babies, children, and women in particular. For instance, in the 1968 movie *Rosemary's Baby*, a young, somewhat naïve woman gradually finds out that she is part of an occultist conspiracy, which includes her husband and neighbors, and that she has been made pregnant by Satan. The film *The Exorcist* (1973) features a child possessed by the devil, spitting green sulfur and shouting profanities at her mother and the Catholic priest trying to save her. In *The Omen* (1976), a politician and his wife adopt a boy named Damian, who starts killing people when he reaches the age of five. He proves to be the anti-Christ himself. Most notable, in the movie *The Wickerman* (1973), a policeman investigates a young girl's disappearance on an isolated Scottish island where Pagan folklore and rituals still prevail. In solving the mystery, the film unveils the horrifying truth about this ancient, non-Christian, and "barbaric" Pagan community, ending with a human sacrifice. Such movies demonstrate how, in the 1970s, NRMs, particularly non-Christian forms of Paganism and occultism, were framed as the horrifying, irrational Other of modern (Christian) society and civilization – quite literally as a folk devil. Such movies thus functioned as an effective trope to consolidate and strengthen the boundaries between "good" Christianity and rational modernity, on the one hand, and "bad" pagan religion and irrationality, on the other.

Although there are still examples of films in which paganism is presented as evil in folk horror (e.g., *The Witch* [2015] or *Midsommar* [2019]), we have witnessed a change, or even a reversal, of this moral stance over the last decades. Particularly popular horror TV series and sitcoms in the 1990s, such as *Buffy the Vampire Slayer* (1997–2003), *Charmed* (1998–2006), and *Sabrina the Teenage Witch* (1996–2003), reflect and shape a more positive perspective on Paganism, occultism, and magic. In these series, typically female protagonists are engaged with evil as well as good supernatural creatures. They possess spiritual powers, practice magic, and use this in their battle against wicked forces. Paganism, in this frame, is considered empowering. Another telling example of the popularization and normalization of magic is, of course, *Harry Potter* – particularly the film series, based on the widely read novels of J. K. Rowling that came out in eight films between 2001 and 2011. Popular fantasy narratives like these, Feldt (2016) argues, relocate magic to the ordinary life-worlds of young people and influence the ways they perceive religion, spirituality, and magic: "Harry Potter has powerfully re-introduced magic and prevalent ideas from contemporary magical milieus, along with other religious fragments and a teleological, purposeful world, into the mainstream of the Western collective imaginary" (Feldt, 2016: 109–10).

This normalization of paganism, Witchcraft, and magic in popular culture has, of course, not gone uncontested in conservative Christian circles. Many have denounced it as morally harmful and advocated the banning of such media texts (Feldt, 2016: 109–10). On the other hand, it cannot be denied that their proliferation contributed much to the appeal and growth of NRMs like Paganism, Wicca, and Witchcraft among teenagers in the United States, allegedly "spark[ing] continent-wide interest in witchcraft and award[ing] the official Hollywood stamp of 'cool'" (Partridge, 2004: 131). In addition, Gothic horror movies like *Interview with a Vampire* (1994), featuring famous actors like Brad Pitt, Tom Cruise, and Christian Slater, humanized vampires as figures experiencing pain, suffering, and existential crises. Instead of evoking disgust and fear, these dark mythical creatures allowed audiences to identify with their anguish. Even Satanism – once feared in the form of the Church of Satan set up by Anton LaVey (1930–1997) in 1966 and culminating in "satanic panic" in the 1980s (Laycock, 2024: 55) – has come to be framed in popular culture as a constructive symbol of rebelliousness (Partridge, 2004).

In addition, science fiction films like *Star Wars* (1977) and *The Matrix* (1999) feature Pagan and spiritual themes. *Star Wars* introduced The Force: an invisible, immanent, and all-pervading power that special individuals – particularly "the Jedi" – can harness for good or evil. In that sense, "*Star Wars* lured its viewers away from a Christian worldview and introduced them to a 'New Age' system of belief" (Partridge, 2004: 120). Caputo (2001: 79, 85) considers the movie a "reproduction of elemental mythic structures," acknowledging that the "metaphysics of Star Wars is monistic." Furthermore, Possamai (2005) points out that the *Star Wars* worldview spawned the fiction-based NRM of "Jediism," the followers of which consider the movie series to be serving as a latter-day holy text. The classic film *The Matrix* similarly plays with both technologically enhanced (trans)human superpowers and esotericism, Buddhism, and Asian-mystical speculations about the ontological status of reality (Yeffeth, 2003). Having analyzed these and other forms of "invented religions" in film, television series, and popular culture, Cusack concludes that both "Matrixism and Jediism are evidence of the undiminished narrative power of (filmic) science fiction to inspire religion in the twenty-first century" (2010: 131).

Overall, it is clear that the Romantic-religious worldviews of NRMs, once demonized in mainstream media, have lost much of their negative status and stigma. Indeed, Partridge observes the rise of "popular occulture" (2004) at the expense of Christian culture. He builds on Colin Campbell's (2002 [1972]) "cultic milieu" concept, which relativizes the boundaries between society on the one hand and sects, cults, and NRMs on the other, thus installing epistemological individualism and spiritual eclecticism as the new norms. Arguing that "occulture is ... a resource on which people draw, a reservoir of ideas, beliefs, practices and symbols," Partridge's (2004: 84) analysis leads him to the conclusion that we are witnessing a "re-enchantment of the West" due to "the center of spiritual gravity . . . moving away from Judeo-Christian theology to the eclecticism of occulture" (Partridge, 2004: 128). Crucially, then, "occulture" is not just appropriated in a few marginal books, movies, or series, but has become a well-established and fully institutionalized genre in the culture industries, with Paganism being abundantly mediatized, commodified, and popularized. The genre of fantasy fiction, for example, constitutes the pinnacle of this "mediatized paganism" (Aupers, 2013).

## Pagan Fantasy in the Culture Industry

The affinity between fantasy fiction and Paganism is established in a number of studies (Luhrmann, 1991 [1989]; Adler, 1997[1986]; Berger, 1999). Paganism is, first of all, a "literary culture," with "potential magicians enter[ing] magic through browsing in bookstores" (Luhrmann, 1991 [1989]: 238). Pagans ground their worldview in books claiming objectivity, like historical works on Greek mythology, Celtic lore, Eleusian mysteries, folklore studies, or anthropological works on witchcraft or shamanism. But they also freely use fictional works to design and legitimate their own traditions (Luhrmann, 1991 [1989]). This use of fiction is, for instance, demonstrated by the Pagan appropriation of *Witchcraft Today* (1954) – a book written by Gerald Gardner (1884–1964), the founder of the Wicca movement, which is known to be a fictional ethnography. Another example is The Church of All Worlds, an American Pagan movement founded in the 1960s around Robert Heinlein's science fiction novel *Stranger in a Strange Land* (1961). The Pagan movement self-consciously and playfully creates its own "mythopoeic history" in a modern, disenchanted or "myth-impoverished" world (Luhrmann 1991 [1989]: 238, 241).

Most influential in shaping the Pagan imagination is what is called "high fantasy." In one of the early studies on Paganism in the United States, Adler (1986: 285) concludes that "science fiction and fantasy probably come closer than any other literature to systematically exploring the central concerns of Neo-Pagans and Witches." The genre of fantasy typically features a Romantic critique of modernity while simultaneously offering monistic, nature-based forms of myth and spirituality as meaningful alternatives. Notable, in this respect, is the work of J. R. R. Tolkien (1892–1973) – an Oxford University professor who specialized in medieval English language and literature, best known for writing *The Hobbit* (1937) and the famous *Lord of the Rings* (*LoTR*) trilogy that was originally published in 1954 (*The Fellowship of the Ring*) and 1955 (*The Two Towers* and *The Return of the King* respectively). Together with C. S. Lewis, Owen Barfield, and other fantasy writers that united in an informal Oxford-based group called the "Inklings," Tolkien is generally considered the founder of high fantasy. Although he was a Roman Catholic, his work and its underlying worldview were deeply informed by Pagan traditions. *LoTR* (Tolkien, 1954[1987]) takes place in "Middle Earth," a fictional world inspired by the Middle Ages, which is inhabited by hobbits, orcs, elves, and wizards, each with their own habits, songs, languages, beliefs, and rituals. *LoTR* is largely based on Norse mythology and embraces a "polytheistic-cum-animist cosmology of 'natural magic'" (Curry, 1998: 28).

These premodern religious worldviews are important, Tolkien felt, because he believed that "the 'war' against mystery and magic by modernity urgently requires a re-enchantment of the world, which a sense of Earth-mysteries is much better placed to offer than a single transcendent deity" (Curry, 1998: 28–9). The fiction of *LoTR* (Tolkien, 1954[1987]) both reflects and constitutes this "Neopagan reverence for nature," which became increasingly popular in the 1960s and 1970s at the expense of Christianity. It embodied the Romantic underpinnings of the countercultural NRMs at the time, emphasizing monism, experience, and expressivism. "Taken together," Curry states, *LoTR* and high fantasy constitute "radical nostalgia" for a premodern world and "a remedy for pathological modernity in a nutshell: namely the resacralization (or re-enchantment) of experienced and living nature, including human nature" (1998: 25, 29). In his famous essay *On Fairy Stories*, Tolkien (2001 [1938]) himself explained that the genre of high fantasy, not unlike religion, provides a universal truth and "consolation" vis-à-vis human suffering; nevertheless, he insisted that the creation of a mythical "secondary world" filled with nature-based religion and spirituality is not a frivolous matter. A good mythmaker, he argues, "makes a secondary world that your mind can enter. Inside it, what he relates to is 'true': it accords with the laws of that world" (Tolkien, 2001 [1938]: 12).

The evolution of the public reception of *LoTR* is indicative of the normalization of the Pagan worldview and its institutionalization in the culture industry. When first published in 1954/1955, it was negatively reviewed by the literary world, with one reviewer even denouncing it as "juvenile trash" (cited in Curry, 1998: 13). However, due to its Romantic critique of modern institutions and plea for nature-based spirituality and lived experience, it became a bestseller in the counterculture of the 1960s and 1970s. Indeed, *LoTR* resonated with the Romantic ideals of the counterculture. It inspired various Pagan movements and spiritual communities modeled after "The Shire" (the Hobbits' fictional country), and it motivated political activists and hippies to launch the political campaign *Frodo for President* (Davidsen, 2014: 185–204). Saying, as Curry (1998: 13) does, that "Tolkien has outlived the counter-culture in which he first flourished" is an understatement. By now, over 600 million copies of the trilogy have been sold and its successful film trilogy, directed by Peter Jackson, has become a landmark in Hollywood. *The Fellowship of the Ring* (2001), *The Two Towers* (2002), and *The Return of the King* (2003) were crucial to bringing high fantasy to a wide mainstream audience in audiovisual format. *LoTR*'s cultural legacy continues to live on in fantasy films and TV series like HBO's *Game of Thrones* (2011–2019), *House of the Dragon* (2022–2024), or *The Chronicles of Narnia* (2005–2010). Campbell acknowledges the pivotal role of the fantasy genre in animating what he calls the "mythopoeic culture" that emerged in the countercultural 1960s and 1970s, sensitizing people to post-Christian, alternative forms of religion and spirituality:

> [F]antasy literature has now become a dominant force in modern fiction ... but also in film, television, and computer games, such that a virtual tidal wave of stories embodying myths or set in mythic worlds has swept through the modern culture of the West. One can conclude from this that we now live in a mythopoeic culture, one in which stories about supernatural beings and events are continually being created ... and eagerly consumed. (Campbell, 2007: 329)

In the twenty-first century, Pagan narratives have become trans-medial due to their migration from mass media formats – literature, film, and TV series – to computer games that invite their players to escape modern life by actively immersing themselves in virtual fantasy worlds that are brimming with magic, mysticism, and the supernatural. Instead of passively reading texts or watching movies and television, gamers can now actively participate in such worlds through role-playing and the formation of social communities. Digital games exemplify what can be called the "spiritual experience economy" (Aupers, 2012).

Already in the 1970s, early game designers drew inspiration from the work of Tolkien and the fantasy genre (Turkle, 2002; Bartle, 2004). As Davis (1999 [1998]: 208) observes, "The *Lord of the Rings* didn't just make you want to escape in another world; it made you want to build your own." Sherry Turkle (2002: 18) confirms: "The personal computer movement of the 1970s and 1980s was deeply immersed in Tolkien and translated his fantasy worlds into hugely popular (and enduring) role-playing games." From board games like *Dungeons and Dragons* (1972) to the first digital multiplayer games like *Adventure* (1976) and countless text-based role-playing games like *The Shire* (1979), *Ringen* (1979), *Lord of the Rings* (1981), *LORD* (1981), *Ring of Doom* (1983), *Ringmaster* (1984), *The Mines of Moria* (1985), *Bilbo* (1989), *The Balrogian Trilogy* (1989), and *Elendor* (1991) – the Pagan spirituality of *LoTR* was, and still is, highly influential in the game industry. In that sense, Richard Bartle (2004: 61–2), one of the most influential designers in the field of online gaming, stated, "The single most important influence on virtual worlds from fiction is J. R. R. Tolkien's The Lord of the Rings trilogy."

Narratives featuring Romantic (Pagan) religion and spirituality are particularly prevalent in Massive Multiplayer Online Role-Playing Games (MMORPGs). The first generation of these online games, developed in the 1990s and 2000s, include *Ultima Online* (1997), *Everquest* (1999), *Dark Age of Camelot* (2001), and *World of Warcraft* (2004). As the producers of *World of Warcraft* comment in their advertisements: "A world awaits ... Descend into the *World of Warcraft* and join thousands of mighty heroes in an online world of myth, magic and limitless adventure ... An infinity of experiences await. So what are you waiting for?" The main difference between these and console games (those played on an Xbox or PlayStation) is that these online environments facilitate interactive role-playing and collective community building in an audiovisual space inhabited by multiple players, often thousands of them. Indeed, MMORPGs are not just games, but interactive worlds that boast lived experiences. Given the fantasy content of these games, Rushkoff (1996: 127) argues, they afford a "world of paganism" – otherworldly environments that "include pagan rituals, magic spells, interdimensional travel, mysterious keys, objects with totemic powers, companion animals." Through role-play, gamers can freely experiment with Pagan worldviews, animism, and polytheism and, in doing so, reflect on their value for their own (religious) identity (Schaap & Aupers, 2017). They can also "play a religious Other" and start to empathize with religious-spiritual worldviews that are not their own (De Wildt & Aupers, 2019). Two examples of MMORPGs demonstrate the possibilities that religious role-play games afford. In *Everquest*, one can become a sorcerer, warlock, wizard, enchanter, illusionist, coercer, summoner, necromancer, conjurer, druid, warden, fury, shaman, defiler, or mystic. In *Dark Age of Camelot*, one can become a cabalist, rune master, bone dancer, spirit master, healer, bard, mentalist, or animist. All of these player roles are well defined in their instructions and come with different spiritual qualities and rituals. For instance, if you choose to be a shaman, you can do the following according to the manual of *World of Warcraft*:

> The shaman is an effective spell caster, but can also fight extremely well with mace and staff. The shaman's line-of-spirit spells enables it to perform a variety of useful non-combat actions. It can resurrect allies, turn into a ghost wolf for increased movements, or instantly teleport to town. The shamans' unique power is totems. Totems are spiritual objects that a shaman must earn through questing. Resurrecting the dead, healing, draining souls, summoning spirits, telekinesis, teleport, paralyze, creating energy bolts, becoming invisible, shape shifting, causing earthquakes; the spells and possibilities to perform magic in the games are various. (cited in Aupers, 2013)

In addition to role-playing, players can choose clans, tribes, or guilds to connect and collectively celebrate their adopted beliefs. In *World of Warcraft*, for instance, one can choose to join the Church of the Holy Light, a full-fledged religious organization with a council of bishops, priests, and approximately 800,000 members who do not adhere to a transcendent God, but embrace a spiritual force that permeates everything. Much like The Force in *Star Wars*, this Holy Light enhances human power and advocates treading the "path of the three virtues." This demonstrates the fact that whereas Paganism plays the most prominent role in computer games, it is complemented with countless other forms of religiosity. Religious eclecticism is indeed the norm in game design, with producers freely drawing on "fiction-based religion" as well as "history-based religion" (Davidsen, 2014). Twenty-first-century games such as *Age of Mythology* (2002), *Assasins Creed* (2007–2023), *Final Fantasy* (1987–2023), *Ōkami* (2006), *Prince of Persia* (1989–2024), *Zelda: Breath of the Wild* (2017), and myriad others have their roots in Greek, Egyptian, Norse, Chinese, Shinto, Zoroastrian, and other theo-mythologies (De Wildt & Aupers, 2021). Despite the fictional character of their narratives, these games are often considered "real" by their audiences and devoted fans, either because they are decoded in a nonliteral, existential, or symbolic fashion (Campbell, 2007), or because they are subjectively experienced *as* real (Aupers, 2012). Moreover, they often provide resources to develop "pop theologies" in online discussions (De Wildt & Aupers, 2019) or even build a full-fledged "invented religion" (Cusack, 2010), "fiction-based religion" (Davidsen, 2014), or "hyper-real religion" (Possamai, 2005).

In conclusion, Paganism is now omnipresent in media – in books, films, TV series, as well as online games. Particularly through high fantasy it has entered the culture industry as a stable and institutionalized genre available to a large, diverse audience. This development is as ironic as it is paradoxical. Like all countercultural NRMs, Paganism is intrinsically critical of the modern world of science, technology, and capitalist consumption. And yet, it is now repackaged, produced, and consumed in a fully mediatized and commodified context. Online games produced by Sony, Microsoft, Blizzard Entertainment, and other companies in the game industry, literally sell Pagan worlds of mystery, magic, and spirituality. One game designer goes as far as to say that at a conference on videogames "spiritual experiences are, in fact, our business" (Moriarty, 1993, cited in Aupers, 2012).

This is, of course, not an entirely new development. Sociologists of religion have characterized the new religiosities that play out beyond the Christian churches as governed by the logic of the market: as a "market of ultimate significance" (Luckmann, 1967), a "client and audience cult" (Stark &

Bainbridge, 1985) or even a "commodification of spirituality" (Carette & King, 2004). The Paganism that is endemic to computer games does not merely entail a commodification of spirituality, however, but also indicates a "spiritualization of commodities" (Aupers, 2012). In what has been called the "experience economy" (Pine & Gilmore, 1999), esotericism, Paganism, magic, and mysticism drive a narrative that promises to enrich consumers' personal lives. According to Lau (2000: 9), such religious narratives do not simply "circle back to an imagined past existing prior to industrialization, a past epitomized by references to more integrated relationships and the interconnectedness of all living things," but also promise to heal "the anxieties about risk society and the diseases of modernity."

This paradox of seeking (spiritual) salvation in a fully mediatized, technological, and commodified context can be taken one step further with the rise and popularity of what may be called "NRMs 2.0" in the heart of the modern tech industry: Silicon Valley.

## NRMs in Silicon Valley

In his global bestseller, *Homo Deus: A Brief History of Tomorrow*, the historian and philosopher Yuval Noah Harari writes, "The new religions are unlikely to emerge from the caves of Afghanistan or from the madrasas of the Middle East. Rather, they will emerge from research laboratories (Harari, 2016: 351). Spiritual salvation, Harari contends, is no longer monopolized by traditional religion from East or West. "Despite all the talk of radical Islam and Christian fundamentalism," he observes, "the most interesting place in the world from a religious perspective is not the Islamic State or the Bible Belt, but Silicon Valley. That's where high-tech gurus are brewing for us brave new religions that have nothing to do with God, and everything to do with technology" (Harari, 2016: 351).

We can consider the online game worlds discussed earlier as examples of such "brave new religions." Highly advanced computer technology – complex software programs, algorithms, animations, graphics, and pixels – here opens up the possibility to immerse players in premodern religions and provide them with supernatural powers. Yet, Harari refers not so much to religious narratives *in* virtual worlds but rather to a religion *of* digital technology, that is, to NRMs in which participants conceive advanced digital worlds as capable of enhancing human potential and bringing spiritual salvation. In a variation on the famous slogan of Marshall McLuhan: such NRMs hold that the medium itself is the (religious) message.

To be sure, such technologically enhanced new religions have a long history in Western, Christian culture (Noble, 1999 [1997]), but most relevant for our analysis is the fact that contemporary varieties can be traced back to the Romantic counterculture of the 1960s. Extending his analysis of the counterculture (1968), Theodore Roszak noted in *From Satori to Silicon Valley* (2000) that the countercultural milieu of the 1960s did *not* unambiguously consider technology alienating. The counterculture certainly featured nature-celebrating Romantics and NRMs that adopted a strict luddite, anti-technological stance. Those concerned considered high-tech part and parcel of "the system" and understood giant mainframe computers – developed and owned by large corporations like IBM, the state, and the military – as basically incompatible with spirituality. At the same time, however, the counterculture also featured a typically unacknowledged wing of technophiles – Romantic hippies, spiritual hackers, and programmers who similarly resisted "the system" yet considered personalized computer technology a powerful tool of salvation rather than alienation (e.g., Rushkoff, 1994; Aupers, Houtman & Pels, 2008; Aupers, 2009; Aupers & Houtman, 2010). This technophile wing of the counterculture has given rise to countless new NRMs in Silicon Valley, all based on the same Romantic underpinnings as New Age, the Human Potential Movement, and Paganism. The main difference is that these "NRMs 2.0" have revised ontological understandings of (human) nature by embracing technology as a source of spiritual experience and salvation. As Davis (1999 [1998]: 119) argues, such new NRMs in Silicon Valley "reject the pastel visions of the New Age" and "extol a new strain of technological perfectionism, one that comes across as a brain-jacked, hardheaded revision of the human potential movement."

Key players in the California spiritual milieu responsible for the development of such "high-tech New Age" (Hanegraaff, 1996: 11) were people like Ken Kesey, Terrence McKenna and, most notably, Timothy Leary. Their early experiments with hallucinogenic drugs as a tool for self-knowledge and spirituality go hand in hand with an interest in digital technology. During the 1980s and 1990s, Leary argued already that "hard technology" may in fact promise a more effective avenue toward spiritual experience and salvation than "soft techniques" like yoga, tai chi, chakra healing, or even mind-expanding drugs. He compared the personal computer to LSD (e.g., Dery, 1996), proposed to move from "psychedelia" to "cyberdelia," and suggested that one can escape an "alienating" and "repressive" modern society by immersing oneself in the new otherworldly realm of cyberspace that computer networks were opening up at the time:

> Recite to yourself some of the traditional attributes of the word "spiritual": mythic, magical, ethereal, incorporeal, intangible, non-material, disembodied, ideal, platonic. Is that not a definition of the electronic-digital? ... These "spiritual" realms, over centuries imagined, may, perhaps, now be realized!
> (in Dery, 1996)

Leary was no exception in the 1990s. The new technologies of the personal computer, internet, and the World Wide Web rapidly gave rise to "counter culture 2.0" (Dery, 1996) or "cyberian counterculture" (Rushkoff, 1994: 6–7). Its aficionados in the San Francisco Bay Area were countercultural hippies, New Agers, and self-proclaimed techno-pagans and spiritual hackers working in the domain of high-tech – all sharing ideas about the role of digital technology in extending human potential and the coming of a technology-enhanced New Age. Douglas Rushkoff summarizes:

> The mission of the cyberian counterculture of the 1990s, armed with new technologies, familiar with cyberspace and daring enough to explore unmapped realms of consciousness, is to rechoose reality consciously and purposefully. Cyberians are not just exploring the next dimension; they are working to create it. (Rushkoff, 1994, 6–7)

More than the fantasy genre, it was science fiction that inspired religious-spiritual imaginations of cyberspace and virtual reality in this period. Most notable was the work of cyberpunk authors like William Gibson (who coined the concept "cyberspace"), Vernor Vinge ("The Other Plane"), and Neal Stephenson ("The Metaverse"). In his novel *Neuromancer* (1995 [1984]), Gibson famously described a future society in which the protagonist "lived for the bodiless exultation [sic] of cyberspace," experiencing ordinary life and material reality as "the fall" and the body as "meat" or "a prison of flesh" (Gibson, 1995 [1984]: 12). Hackers, internet gurus, writers, and journalists made cyberspace and virtual reality the staple of a romantic-spiritual discourse in the technophile wing of the counterculture in the San Francisco Bay Area. The discourse was featured in countercultural journals and magazines like the *New Earth Catalogue* (founded by Stewart Brand), *Mondo 2000*, and *Wired Magazine*; at raves, multimedia performances, and outdoor festivals like Burning Man in the Nevada desert, where art, psychedelics, and technology are ritualized to transform human consciousness; and at seminars like *MindState* or *Technology and Transcendence* (Zandbergen, 2011). Such events in the 1990s imagined cyberspace as an otherworldly and disembodied space of spiritual liberation: a "paradise" where we "will all be angels, and for eternity!" (Stenger 1992 [1991]: 52), a "new Jerusalem" (Benedikt 1992 [1991]: 14), indeed a "technological substitute of the Christian space of heaven" (Wertheim 1999: 16).

This techno-spirituality was not a short-lived trend in the 1990s, but has become a permanent feature of the culture of Silicon Valley that co-evolves with and is constantly updated by new developments in the domain of technology. Various technology-focused NRMs exemplify this. The Raelian movement, founded in 1974 by Claude Vorilhon (b. 1946), had traditionally held that humans are genetically engineered by space aliens (the Elohim), but has more recently come to seek salvation and eternal life through cloning, biotechnology, and nanotechnology (Machado, 2010). The so-called "Extropians," founded by the philosopher Max More in 1988 and represented in the *World Transhumanist Association* (1998) and the *Journal of Transhumanism* (1998), strive for human enhancement and eternal life by investigating developments in the fields of artificial intelligence, nanotechnology, genetic engineering, robotics, and space exploration.

Much of this type of techno-spirituality falls under the heading of trans- or posthumanism (Fukuyama, 2002; Geraci, 2010; Harari, 2016). Unlike nature-oriented NRMs, these new movements focus not so much on "who we really are" or "how we can become who we really are," but rather adopt a constructivist perspective that foregrounds "what we can become." Here humanistic forms of spirituality, so characteristic of Paganism, the Human Potential Movement, and the New Age, are transformed into posthumanistic ones. This discourse does not hold that *we are essentially Gods*, hidden in the deeper layers of our beings, but rather that *we can become like (immortal) Gods* through the use of new technology. It is from this perspective that Harari writes about the creation of *Homo Deus* (2016). Ray Kurzweil – probably the most outspoken and influential posthumanist in the milieu – argues in *Transcendent Man* (Ptolemy, 2009), the documentary about his life and work: "Does God exist? I would say, 'Not yet'."

Kurzweil is not a marginal figure in Silicon Valley. He is a respected and influential computer scientist, well known for inventing the first print-to-speech reading machine and for his work on life-extension as director at Google's spin-off company Calico since 2012. In his bestselling books *The Age of Spiritual Machines: When Computers Exceed Human Intelligence* (1999) and *The Singularity Is Near* (2005), he optimistically prophesizes the ultimate promises of biotechnology, information communication technology, and artificial intelligence, that is, radical improvements in human cognition, health, and wellbeing. Kurzweil doesn't stop at pointing out these mundane advantages. He predicts that humans will ultimately merge with technology so as to become, literally, supernatural creatures that transcend the human condition, plagued as it has traditionally been by misfortune, illness, and death. Together with a handful of pioneers in the fields of techno-science – for example, Hans Moravec (robotics), Eric Drexler (co-founder of nanotechology), and the late Marvin Minsky (cognitive science, co-founder of AI) – Kurzweil prefigures variegated technologies of salvation, the most spectacular one being "storing consciousness into a computer" or "uploading it to cyberspace" so as to attain immortality (Aupers & Houtman, 2010; Geraci, 2010). Based on radical materialist interpretations of the brain and human consciousness as being "mere patterns of information" that can be copied, saved, and transferred to a computer, robot, or the Internet, trans- or posthumanists hold that we can live forever online like disembodied and immortal gods, angels, or spiritual entities.

Various NRMs have formed around these posthumanist dreams in online groups (see Aupers, 2009; Geraci, 2010), like the Society for Universal Immortalism, according to which, "We have a soul and it's informational by nature." The I-will-be-God theme figures prominently among Silicon Valley trans- and posthumanists. David, an aerospace engineer and programmer, who talks about his conversion from Christian fundamentalism to a believer in this new tech-religion, hopes to get "rid of the meat" and "set the spirit free." Eric, a producer of digital chips in a Silicon Valley factory, muses about his experiences once his consciousness has been uploaded: "Here I am in a computer. And I am faster, I could be transmitted across the universe as bits, instead of a body. This maps out the notion of being souls, spiritual entities." An Extropian programmer referring to himself as Reason, finally, comments:

> We're becoming Gods as soon as we make ourselves the way we want. The interesting part for me is not the physical world. I will eventually leave my body behind. But only because it limits my independence. . . . The ability for me to become more than human, much more than human, until a point where I cannot even conceive what I will become. I will become a God! Everyone who wants to become a God will become a God. You sit there and just can't wrap your head around it but it's obviously the way to go. It's inevitable. If you choose that path. (Cited in Aupers, 2009)

All of the foregoing demonstrates how the Romantic logic of the NRMs no longer arouses concern or panic, but has become mediatized, commodified, and technologized. First of all, it has become a mainstay in popular (oc)culture since at least the 1990s. Films and TV series use its signs and symbols as tropes to hack out an imaginary space of ultimate meaning in juxtaposition to Christianity and the alienations of late-modern life. It has meanwhile also become prominent in online computer games that allow players to (inter)actively immerse themselves in virtual worlds of magical possibilities and enchantment. The contemporary culture industry thus paradoxically thrives on the religious logic of NRMs that initially opposed rationalization, capitalism, and mass media as alienating forces. The irony of this has not gone unnoticed. Over the last decades of the twentieth century, Frank (1998) notes, capitalist corporations have co-opted countercultural Romanticism in a relentless "conquest of cool." In a similar vein, Heath and Potter point out that markets, brands, and advertisements nowadays target the "rebellious consumer" since "the critique of mass society has been one of the most powerful forces driving consumerism for the past forty years" (2004: 98).

This relocation of the countercultural logic of NRMs to the heart of modern society plays out not least in Silicon Valley, where digital technologies – from the personal computer in the 1970s, the internet and cyberspace in the 1990s, to contemporary nanotechnology, robotics, Artificial Intelligence and biotechnology – are no longer considered alienating, but seen as tools to afford spiritual experience and re-enchantment. Whether we are witnessing veritable "brave new religions" of the future (Harari, 2016) or "the creation of a religion for the Third Millennium," as VR-specialist Giulio Prisco calls it (in Geraci, 2010: 87), remains to be seen. What is important in the context of this Element, is that the countercultural logic of the NRMs has permeated Silicon Valley's high-tech industry, where it has spurred NRMs 2.0 that have made the digital medium the spiritual message for the new millennium.

## Conclusion

In this Element we have analyzed the underlying cultural logic of the variegated NRMs that have emerged since the 1950s and that particularly bloomed in the 1960s and 1970s. Our main argument in the first part (Sections 1 and 2) is that Romanticism or, more precisely, the revived Romantic worldview of the counterculture in that period, supplied their ideology and appeal. We demonstrated that emphasizing the uniqueness of each NRM and pointing out the diversity of the new "market of ultimate significance" (Luckman, 1967) or a "postmodern" fragmentation of religion (Lyon, 2000), makes the major influence of the "grand narrative" of Romanticism on NRMs invisible. This Romantic spirit, however, is precisely why young, middle-class, baby boomers who felt disenchanted with institutional religion and alienated by the rationality of industrialism, science, and technocratic systems – found solace in NRMs. In all their difference and diversity, NRMs offered a Romantic type of religion that matched young people's countercultural critique and hunger for natural living, spiritual experience, and self-expression. Based on our analysis, we therefore conclude that it is feasible to refer to New Religious Movements (NRMs) as Romantic Religious Movements (RRMs).

Even though the rise and prominence of these RRMs in the 1960s challenges sociological theories about modernization and its progressive rationalization, secularization, and disenchantment, the development can surely be explained by such classical sociological theories as well. These theories already pointed out the unforeseen side effects of modernization – from Weber's problems of meaning in a bureaucratic, rationalized, and "disenchanted world"; to Durkheim's "anomie" in a society that is socially disintegrating and governed by a distant State; to Marx's "alienation" in a capitalist system of production and consumption. It is exactly these "maladies of modernity" (Zijderveld, 2000) that were acutely experienced by baby boomers in the 1960s and that motivated the formation and appeal of these RRMs in the first place. Weber already witnessed popular Romantic religious initiatives at the turn of the nineteenth and twentieth centuries in the city of Heidelberg, like Theosophy, Spiritualism or Bergson's philosophy of life. However, he failed to theorize about their potential implications (Aupers & Houtman, 2010). In *Science as Vocation* (1948 [1919]), Weber even morally dismissed such initiatives bluntly as "weakness," "humbug," and "self-deception," and added that one should "bear the fate of the times like a man" (149). But given his principled, non-deterministic perspective on history, Weber kept open a small backdoor for a re-enchantment in/of the iron cage of modern science, capitalism, rational rules, and procedures. After all, "No one knows who will live in this cage in the future, or whether at the end of this tremendous development entirely new prophets will arise" (2005 [1904/05]): 182).

The RRMs of the 1960s and 1970s exemplified this re-enchantment, their prophets explicitly preaching against modern systems *and* traditional Christian churches alike. While neither Weber nor these prophets themselves expected this, the Romantic spirit of these NRMs has meanwhile become part of the modern mainstream, as demonstrated in the second part of our analysis (Sections 3 and 4). The ideologies of the RRMs – once distinctly rebellious and principally counter-cultural – have now come to deeply penetrate quintessential modern institutions. As our analysis demonstrates, New Age spirituality has become institutionalized in health care and is put to work in commercial business organizations; Paganism has become mediatized and commodified in the culture industry of films, TV series, and online games; and NRMs in Silicon Valley now promise spiritual experience and re-enchantment through the use of digital technology. This analysis thus shows that the Romantic spirit does not necessarily operate *against* modernity but should instead be considered a spirit *of* modernity. This is the core paradox thematized in this Element: the Romantic spirit of NRMs, once deeply countercultural, has become a driving ideological force consolidating and strengthening the machineries of late-modern institutions.

How should we evaluate this development? Critical, Neo-Marxist scholars may emphasize that the modern appropriation of the Romantic spirit has become an ideology concealing the bare, cold mechanisms of modern capitalism that keep people, workers and consumers alike, in a false/happy consciousness. Through the diffusion of this ideology, people remain detached, deeply Zen, engaged with their inner selves, mindful perhaps, but it is precisely this state of mind that keeps them from being critical of the system within which they work and consume (e.g., Lau, 2000; Jain, 2014; Kucinskas, 2018). To the contrary, it makes them work even harder and consume even more. The first generation of countercultural baby boomers – those who fiercely "attacked the power structure of modern systems" (Roszak, 1995 [1969]: xxxi) – would without doubt have considered this a sell-out: a bankruptcy of Romantic ideals, a loss of revolutionary potential, and an end to the promises of a spiritual New Age.

However, such a critical evaluation "brings us to the world of judgements of value and of faith, with which this purely historical discussion need not to be burdened," as Weber observes at the end of *The Protestant Ethic and the Spirit of Capitalism* (2005 [1904/05]): 182). More than anything else, our analysis demonstrates the "unanticipated consequences of purposive social action" (Merton, 1936) and "the irony of history" (Campbell, 1987: 210) that is so characteristic of Weber's work. Like the Protestants in the sixteenth century who piously embraced an inner-worldly religious ethic of discipline, soberness, and hard work to prove their worth to a transcendent God, these RRMs piously pursued religious-cultural change for the sake of religious-cultural change. Those engaged in revolutionary writings, investing in Asian mystic traditions, practicing Pagan magic in nature, or experiencing God in Christian Charismatic movements were all motivated by "a dissenting sensibility as old as the lament that the Romantic poets had once raised against the Dark Satanic Mills" (Roszak, 1995 [1969]: xiv). Not unlike the early Protestants, then, the leaders and participants of the RRMs in the counterculture neither hoped nor expected that their actions would end up supporting the power structures of modern institutions. And yet, this is what they did.

# References

Adler, M. (1986 [1997]). *Drawing Down the Moon: Witches, Druids, Godess-Worshippers, and Other Pagans in America Today*. Boston, MA: Beacon Press.

Altglas, V. (2014). *From Yoga to Kabbalah: Religious Exoticism and the Logics of Bricolage*. Oxford: Oxford University Press.

Ashmos, D. P. & Duchon, D. (2000). Spirituality at Work: A Conceptualization and Measure. *Journal of Management Inquiry*, 9(2), 134–45.

Aupers, S. (2009). "The Force Is Great": Enchantment and Magic in Silicon Valley. *Masaryk University Journal of Law and Technology*, 3(1), 153–73.

Aupers, S. (2012). Enchantment Inc: Online Gaming between Spiritual Experience and Commodity Fetishism. In D. Houtman & B. Meyer, eds., *Things: Material Religion and the Topography of Divine Spaces*. New York: Fordham University Press, pp. 339–55.

Aupers, S. (2013). A World Awaits: The Meaning of Mediatized Paganism in Online Computer Games. In W. Hofstee & A. van der Kooij, eds., *Religion: Public or Private?* Leiden: Brill, pp. 225–43.

Aupers, S. & Houtman, D. (2006). Beyond the Spiritual Supermarket: The Social and Public Significance of New Age Spirituality. *Journal of Contemporary Religion*, 21(2), 201–22.

Aupers, S. & Houtman, D. (2010). *Religions of Modernity: Relocating the Sacred to the Self and the Digital*. Leiden: Brill.

Aupers, S., Houtman, D., & Pels, P. (2008). Cybergnosis: Technology, Religion and the Secular. In H. de Vries, ed., *Religion: Beyond a Concept*. New York: Fordham University Press, pp. 687–703.

Baer, H. (2004). *Toward an Integrative Medicine: Merging Alternative Therapies with Biomedicine*. Walnut Creek, CA: AltaMira Press.

Barker, E. (1978). Living the Divine Principle: Inside the Reverend Sun Myung Moon's Unification Church in Britain. *Archives de sciences sociales des religions*, 45(1), 75–93.

Barker, E. (1984). *The Making of a Moonie: Choice or Brainwashing?* Oxford: Blackwell.

Barker, E. (2004). Perspective: What We Are Studying. A Sociological Case for Keeping the "*Nova*". *Nova Religio: The Journal of Alternative and Emergent Religions*, 8(1), 88–102.

Barker, E. (2014). The Not-So-New Religious Movements: Changes in "the Cult Scene" over the Past Forty Years. *Temenos*, 50(2), 235–56.

# References

Barkun, M. (2006). *A Culture of Conspiracy: Apocalyptic Visions in Contemporary America*. Berkeley: University of California Press.

Barrett, B., Marchand, L., Scheder, J. et al. (2003). Themes of Holism, Empowerment, Access, and Legitimacy Define Complementary, Alternative, and Integrative Medicine in Relation to Conventional Biomedicine. *Journal of Alternative and Complementary Medicine*, 9(6), 937–47.

Bartle, R. (2004). *Designing Virtual Worlds*. Berkeley, CA: New Riders.

Bell, D. (1976). *The Cultural Contradictions of Capitalism*. New York: Basic Books.

Bellah, R. N. (1976). New Religious Consciousness and the Crisis in Modernity. In R. N. Bellah & C. Y. Glock, eds., *The New Religious Consciousness*. Berkeley: University of California Press, pp. 333–52.

Bellah, R. N. & Glock, C. Y. (1976). *The New Religious Consciousness*. Berkeley: University of California Press.

Bellah, R. N., Madsen, R., Sullivan, W. M., Swidler, A., & Tipton, S. M. (1985). *Habits of the Heart: Individualism and Commitment in American Life*. Berkeley: University of California Press.

Bender, C. (2010). *The New Metaphysicals: Spirituality and the American Religious Imagination*. Chicago, IL: University of Chicago Press.

Benedikt, M. (1992 [1991]). Introduction. In M. Benedikt, ed., *Cyberspace: First Steps*. Cambridge, MA: MIT Press, pp. 1–26.

Berger, H. (1999). *A Community of Witches: Contemporary Neopaganism and Witchcraft in the United States*. Columbia: University of South Carolina Press.

Berger, P. L. (1967). *The Sacred Canopy: Elements of a Sociology of Religion*. Garden City: Doubleday.

Berman, M. (1970). *The Politics of Authenticity: Radical Individualism and the Emergence of Modern Society*. New York: Atheneum.

Bigliardi, S. (2023). *New Religious Movements and Science*. Cambridge: Cambridge University Press.

Blake, W. (1998 [1804]). *Jerusalem*. In R. N. Essick and J. Viscomi, eds., *Milton: A Poem*. Princeton, NJ: Princeton University Press.

Bloom, H. (1992). *The American Religion: The Emergence of the Post-Christian Nation*. New York: Simon & Schuster.

Boltanski, L. & Chiapello, E. (2007). *The New Spirit of Capitalism*. London: Verso.

Bromley, D. G. (2004). Perspective: Wither New Religions Studies? Defining and Shaping a New Area of Study. *Nova Religio: The Journal of Alternative and Emergent Religions*, 8(2), 83–97.

Brown, C. G. (2001). *The Death of Christian Britain: Understanding Secularisation, 1800–2000*. London: Routledge.

Brown, C. G. (2009). *The Death of Christian Britain: Understanding Secularisation 1800–2000*, 2nd ed. London: Routledge.

Brown, C. G. (2024). Holistic Healing and the Re-establishment of Religion in the United States. In D. Houtman & G. Watts, eds., *The Shape of Spirituality: The Public Significance of a New Religious Formation*. New York: Columbia University Press, pp. 87–124.

Campbell, C. (1987). *The Romantic Ethic and the Spirit of Modern Consumerism*. Oxford: Blackwell.

Campbell, C. (2002 [1972]). The Cult, the Cultic Milieu and Secularization. In J. Kaplan & H. Løøv, eds., *The Cultic Milieu: Oppositional Subcultures in an Age of Globalization*. New York: AltaMira Press, pp. 12–25.

Campbell, C. (2007). *The Easternization of the West: A Thematic Account of Cultural Change in the Modern Era*. Boulder, CO: Paradigm.

Caputo, J. (2001). *On Religion*. New York: Routledge.

Carette, J. & King, R. (2004). *Selling Spirituality: The Silent Takeover of Religiosity*. London: Routledge.

Casey, C. (2004). Bureaucracy Re-enchanted? Spirit, Experts and Authority in Organizations. *Organization*, 11(1), 59–79.

Clarke, T. C., Black, L. I., Stussman, B. J., Barnes, P. M., & Nahin, R. L. (2015). Trends in the Use of Complementary Health Approaches Among Adults. United States, 2002–2012. *National Health Statistics Reports*, 79, 1–16.

Cohen, S. (1972). *Folk Devils and Moral Panics: The Creation of the Mods and Rockers*. London: Routledge.

Coleman, S. (2000). *The Globalisation of Charismatic Christianity: Spreading the Gospel of Prosperity*. Cambridge: Cambridge University Press.

Coleridge, S. T. (1834). *Biographia Literaria: Or, Biographical Sketches of My Literary Life and Opinions*. New York: Leavitt, Lord.

Cortois, L., Aupers, S., & Houtman, D. (2018). The Naked Truth: Mindfulness and the Purification of Religion. *Journal of Contemporary Religion*, 33(2), 303–17.

Covey, S. R. (1992 [1989]). *The Seven Habits of Highly Effective People: Restoring the Character Ethic*. London: Simon & Schuster.

Curry, P. (1998). *Defending Middle-Earth: Tolkien, Myth & Modernity*. London: HarperCollins.

Cusack, C. M. (2010). *Invented Religions: Imagination, Fiction and Faith*. Abingdon: Routledge.

Damian-Knight, G. (1986). *The I-Ching on Business and Decision-making*. London: Rider.

Davidsen, M. A. (2013). Fiction-Based Religion: Conceptualising a New Category against History-Based Religion and Fandom. *Culture and Religion*, 14(4), 378–95.

Davidsen, M. A. (2014). The Spiritual Tolkien Milieu: A Study of Fiction-Based Religion. PhD dissertation, Leiden Center for the Study of Religion, University of Leiden, Leiden.

Davis, E. (1999 [1998]). *TechGnosis: Myth, Magic and Mysticism in the Age of Information*. London: Serpent's Tail.

Dawson, L. L. (1998). Anti-Modernism, Modernism, and Postmodernism: Struggling with the Cultural Significance of New Religious Movements. *Sociology of Religion*, 59(2), 131–56.

De Keere, K. (2014). From a Self-Made to an Already-Made Man: A Historical Content Analysis of Professional Advice Literature. *Acta Sociologica*, 57(4), 311–24.

de Wildt, L. & Aupers, S. (2019). Playing the Other: Role-Playing Religion in Videogames. *European Journal of Cultural Studies*, 22(5–6), 867–84.

de Wildt, L. & Aupers, S. (2020). Pop Theology: Forum Discussions on Religion in Videogames. *Information Communication & Society*, 23(10), 1444–62.

de Wildt, L. & Aupers, S. (2021). Eclectic Religion: The Flattening of Religious Cultural Heritage in Videogames. *International Journal of Heritage Studies*, 27(3), 312–30.

Dery, M. (1996). *Escape Velocity: Cyberculture at the End of the Century*. New York: Grove Press.

Ellwood, R. S. (1994). *The Sixties Spiritual Awakening: American Religion Moving from Modern to Postmodern*. New Brunswick, NJ: Rutgers University Press.

Feldt, L. (2016). Harry Potter and Contemporary Magic: Fantasy Literature, Popular Culture, and the Representation of Religion. *Journal of Contemporary Religion*, 31(1), 101–114.

Fisher, P. & Ward, A. (1994). Complementary Medicine in Europe. *British Medical Journal*, 309(6947), 107–11.

Frank, T. (1998). *The Conquest of Cool: Business Culture, Counter Culture, and the Rise of Hip Consumerism*. Chicago, IL: University of Chicago Press.

Fukuyama, F. (2002). *Our Posthuman Future: Consequences of the Biotechnology Revolution*. New York: Farrar, Straus and Giroux.

Fuller, R. C. (2001). *Spiritual but not Religious: Understanding Unchurched America*. New York: Oxford University Press.

Gardner, G. (1954). *Witchcraft Today*. London: Rider.

Garland, R. (1990). *Working and Managing in a New Age*. Brighton: Ivy Books.

Gay, P. (1995). *The Naked Heart: Victoria to Freud*. Oxford: Oxford University Press.

Geraci, R. (2010). *Apocalyptic AI: Visions of Heaven in Robotics, Artificial Intelligence, and Virtual Reality*. New York: Oxford University Press.

Gibson, W. (1984). *Neuromancer*. New York: Ace Books.

Gilmore, J. H. & Pine, B. J. (2007). *Authenticity: What Consumers Really Want*. Boston, MA: Harvard Business Press.

Gog, S., Simionca, A., Bell, A. & Taylor, S. (2020). Spiritualities and neoliberalism: changes and continuities. In Gog, S., Simionca, A., Bell, A. & Taylor, S., eds., *Spirituality, Organization and Neoliberalism: Understanding Lived Experiences*. Cheltenham: Edward Elgar, pp. xxxi–xxxii.

Goode, E. & Ben-Yehuda, N. (1994). *Moral Panics: The Social Construction of Deviance*. Malden, MA: Blackwell.

Gouldner, A. W. (1973). Romanticism and Classicism: Deep Structures in Social Science. In *For Sociology: Renewal and Critique in Sociology Today*. New York: Penguin, pp. 323–66.

Hammer, O. (2001). *Claiming Knowledge: Strategies of Epistemology from Theosophy to the New Age*. Leiden: Brill.

Hammer, O. (2004). Esotericism in New Religious Movements. In J. R. Lewis, ed., *The Oxford Handbook of New Religious Movements*. Oxford: Oxford University Press, pp. 445–65.

Hanegraaff, W. J. (1996). *New Age Religion and Western Culture: Esotericism in the Mirror of Secular Thought*. New York: Brill.

Harari, N. H. (2016). *Homo Deus: A Brief History of Tomorrow*. London: Harvill Secker.

Heath, J. & Potter, A. (2004). *Nation of Rebels: Why Counterculture Became Consumer Culture*. New York: HarperCollins Publishers.

Heelas, P. (1996). *The New Age Movement: The Celebration of the Self and the Sacralization of Modernity*. Oxford: Blackwell.

Heelas, P. (1999). Prosperity and the New Age Movement: The Efficacy of Spiritual Economics. In B. Wilson & J. Cresswell, eds., *New Religious Movements: Challenge and Response*. London: Routledge, pp. 49–78.

Hodkinson, P. (2017). *Media Culture and Society: An Introduction*. London: Sage.

Horkheimer, M. & Adorno, T. W. (2002 [1944]). *Dialectic of Enlightenment: Philosophical Fragments*. Stanford, CA: Stanford University Press.

Houtman, D. (2008). *Op jacht naar de echte werkelijkheid: Dromen over authenticiteit in een wereld zonder fundamenten*. Amsterdam: Pallas.

Houtman, D. & Aupers, S. (2024). A Startling Alliance? Spirituality, Populism, and Anti-Vaccination Protest. In D. Houtman & G. Watts, eds., *The Shape of*

*Spirituality: The Public Significance of a New Religious Formation.* New York: Columbia University Press, pp. 241–66.

Hunt, S., Hamilton, M., & Walter, T. (1997). Introduction: Tongues, Toronto and the Millennium. In S. Hunt, M. Hamilton, & T. Walter, eds., *Charismatic Christianity: Sociological Perspectives.* London: Macmillan Press, pp. 1–16.

Iannaccone, L., Stark, R., & Finke, R. (1998). Rationality and the "Religious Mind." *Economic Inquiry,* 36(3), 373–89.

Inglehart, R. (1977). *The Silent Revolution: Changing Values and Political Styles among Western Publics.* Princeton, NJ: Princeton University Press.

Jain, A. (2014). *Selling Yoga: From Counter Culture to Pop Culture.* Oxford: Oxford University Press.

Kemppainen, L. M., Kemppainen, T. T., Reippainen, J. A., Salmenniemi, S. T., & Vuolanto, P. H. (2018). Use of Complementary and Alternative Medicine in Europe: Health-Related and Sociodemographic Determinants. *Scandinavian Journal of Public Health,* 46(4), 448–55.

Klein, E. & Izzo, J. (1998). *Awakening Corporate Soul: Four Paths to Unleash the Power of People at Work.* Beverley, MA: Fairwinds Press.

Kucinskas, J. (2018). *The Mindful Elite: Mobilizing from the Inside Out.* Oxford: Oxford University Press.

Kurzweil, R. (1999). *The Age of Spiritual Machines: When Computers Exceed Human Intelligence.* New York: Penguin Books.

Kurzweil, R. (2005). *The Singularity Is Near: When Humans Transcend Biology.* New York: Viking.

Lau, K. (2000). *New Age Capitalism: Making Money East of Eden.* Philadelphia: University of Pennsylvania Press.

Laycock, J. P. (2022). *New Religious Movements: The Basics.* London: Routledge.

Laycock, J. P. (2024). *Satanism.* Cambridge: Cambridge University Press.

Lindholm, C. (2008). *Culture and Authenticity.* Oxford: Blackwell.

Løøv, M. (2024). *The New Age Movement.* Cambridge: Cambridge University Press.

LoRusso, D. (2017). *Spirituality, Corporate Culture, and American Business: The Neoliberal Ethic and the Spirit of Global Capital.* New York: Bloomsbury.

Luckmann, T. (1967). *The Invisible Religion: The Problem of Religion in Modern Society.* New York: Macmillan.

Luhrmann, T. M. (1991 [1989]). *Persuasions of the Witch's Craft: Ritual Magic in Contemporary England.* Cambridge, MA: Harvard University Press.

Lyon, D. (2000). *Jesus in Disneyland: Religion in Postmodern Times.* Cambridge: Polity Press.

Machado, C. (2010). Science, Fiction and Religion: About Real and Raelian Possible Worlds. In S. Aupers & D. Houtman, eds., *Religions of Modernity: Relocating the Sacred to the Self and the Digital*. Leiden: Brill, pp. 187–204.

Machado, C. (2012). Brain, Biological Robots and Androids: Prophecies in the Realm of Science Fiction and Religion. In A. Possamai, ed., *Handbook of Hyper-Real Religions*. Leiden: Brill, pp. 85–108.

Marcuse, H. (1964). *One-Dimensional Man: Studies in the Ideology of Advanced Industrial Society*. Boston, MA: Beacon Press.

Martin, B. (1981). *A Sociology of Contemporary Cultural Change*. Oxford: Blackwell.

Martin, D. (2002). *Pentecostalism: The World Their Parish*. Oxford: Blackwell.

Marwick, A. (1998). *The Sixties: Cultural Revolution in Britain, France, Italy, and the United States, c. 1958–c. 1974*. New York: Oxford University Press.

Melton, J. G. (2004). Toward a Definition of "New Religion." *Nova Religio: The Journal of Alternative and Emergent Religions*, 8(1), 73–87.

Merton, R. (1936). The Unanticipated Consequences of Purposive Social Action. *American Sociological Review*, 1(6), 894–904.

Métraux, D. (2013). Soka Gakkai International: The Global Expansion of a Japanese Buddhist Movement. *Religion Compass*, 7(10), 423–32.

Mitroff, I. I. & Denton, E. A. (1999). *A Spiritual Audit of Corporate America: A Hard Look at Spirituality, Religion, and Values in the Workplace*. San Francisco, CA: Jossey-Bass.

Nadesan, M. H. (1999). The Discourses of Corporate Spiritualism and Evangelical Capitalism. *Management Communication Quarterly*, 13(1), 3–42.

Naisbitt, J. & Aburdene, P. (1990). *Mega-Trends 2000*. London: Pan Books.

Noble, D. (1999 [1997]). *The Religion of Technology: The Divinity of Man and the Spirit of Invention*. New York: Penguin Books.

Norris, P. & Inglehart, R. (2004). *Sacred and Secular: Religion and Politics Worldwide*. Cambridge: Cambridge University Press.

Ocejo, R. E. (2017). *Masters of Craft: Old Jobs in the New Urban Economy*. Princeton, NJ: Princeton University Press.

Parsons, T. & Platt, G. M. (1973). *The American University*. Cambridge, MA: Harvard University Press.

Partridge, C. (2004). *The Re-Enchantment of the West*. Vol. I of *Alternative Spiritualities, Sacralization, Popular Culture, Occulture*. London: T&T Clark.

Pine, B. J. & Gilmore, J. H. (1999). *The Experience Economy: Work Is Theatre & Every Business a Stage*. Boston, MA: Harvard Business Press.

Pokorny, L. & Winter, F. (2018). East Asian New Religious Movements: Introductory Remarks. In L. Pokorny & F. Winter, eds., *Handbook of East Asian New Religious Movements*. Leiden: Brill, pp. 3–13.

Poloma, M. (2003). *Main Street Mystics: The Toronto Blessing & Reviving Pentecostalism*. Walnut Creek, CA: AltaMira Press.

Possamai, A. (2005). *Religion and Popular Culture: A Hyper-Real Testament*. Berne: Peter Lang.

Ptolemy, B., dir. (2009). *Transcendent Man: The Life and Ideas of Ray Kurzweil*. 83 minutes. West Los Angeles, CA: Ptolemaic Productions.

Raaphorst, N. & Houtman, D. (2016). A Necessary Evil that Does Not "Really" Cure Disease: The Domestication of Biomedicine by Dutch Holistic General Practitioners. *Health: An Interdisciplinary Journal for the Social Study of Health, Illness and Medicine*, 20(3), 242–57.

Richardson, J. & Introvigne, M. (2007). New Religious Movements, Countermovements, Moral Panics, and the Media. In D. G. Bromley, ed., *Teaching New Religious Movements*. Oxford: Oxford University Press, pp. 91–112.

Robbins, A. (1986). *Unlimited Power: The New Science of Personal Achievement*. London: Simon & Schuster.

Robbins, A. (1991). *Awaken the Giant Within: How to Take Immediate Control of Your Mental, Physical and Financial Destiny*. New York: Free Press.

Robbins, A. (1997 [1989]) *Unlimited Power: The New Science of Personal Achievement*. London, Sydney: Simon & Schuster.

Robbins, T. (2004). Perspective: New Religions and Alternative Religions. *Nova Religio: The Journal of Alternative and Emergent Religions*, 8(3), 104–111.

Rochford, E. Burke (2007). *Hare Krishna Transformed*. New York: New York University Press.

Rogers, C. (1961). *On Becoming a Person*. Boston, MA: Houghton Mifflin.

Roof, W. C. (1999). *Spiritual Marketplace: Baby Boomers and the Remaking of American Religion*. Princeton, NJ: Princeton University Press.

Roszak, T. (1995 [1969]). *The Making of a Counter Culture: Reflections on the Technocratic Society and Its Youthful Opposition*. Berkeley: University of California Press.

Roszak, T. (2000). *From Satori to Silicon Valley*. San Francisco, CA: Don't Call it Frisco Press.

Rothstein, M. (2004). Science and Religion in the New Religions. In J. R. Lewis, ed., *The Oxford Handbook of New Religious Movements*. Oxford: Oxford University Press, pp. 99–118.

Rowan, R. (1986). *The Intuitive Manager*. Boston, MA: Little, Brown and Company.

Rushkoff, D. (1994). *Cyberia: Life in the Trenches of Hyperspace*. San Francisco, CA: HarperCollins.

Rushkoff, D. (1996). *Playing the Future: What We Can Learn From Digital Kids*. New York: Riverhead Trade.

Rutjens, B. T. & van der Lee, R. (2020). Spiritual Skepticism? Heterogeneous Science Skepticism in The Netherlands. *Public Understanding of Science*, 29(3), 335–52.

Rutjens, B. T., Sengupta, N., van der Lee, R. et al. (2022). Science Skepticism across 24 Countries. *Social Psychological and Personality Science*, 13(1), 102–17.

Rutjens, B. T., Zarzeczna, N., & van der Lee, R. (2022). Science Rejection in Greece: Spirituality Predicts Vaccine Scepticism and Low Faith in Science in a Greek Sample. *Public Understanding of Science*, 31(4), 428–36.

Safranski, R. (2014). *Romanticism: A German Affair*. Chicago, IL: Northwestern University Press.

Sappington, A. A. (1991). The Religion/Science Conflict. *Journal for the Scientific Study of Religion*, 30(1), 114–20.

Sawyer, D. & Humes, C. (2023) The Transcendental Meditation Movement. Cambridge: Cambridge University Press.

Schaap, J. & Aupers, S. (2017). Gods in World of Warcraft Exist: Religious Reflexivity and the Quest for Meaning in Online Computer Games. *New Media & Society*, 19(11), 1744–60.

Schmidt, L. E. (2012). *Restless Souls: The Making of American Spirituality*. Berkeley: University of California Press.

Stark, R. & Bainbridge, W. S. (1985). *The Future of Religion: Secularization, Revival and Cult Formation*. Berkeley: University of California Press.

Stenger, N. (1992 [1991]). Mind Is a Leaking Rainbow. In M. Benedikt, ed., *Cyberspace: First Steps*. Cambridge, MA: MIT Press, pp. 49–58.

Stone, D. (1976). The Human Potential Movement. In R. N. Bellah & C. Y. Glock, eds., *The New Religious Consciousness*. Berkeley: University of California Press, pp. 93–115.

Sutcliffe, S. J. (2003). *Children of the New Age: A History of Spiritual Practices*. London: Routledge.

Sutcliffe, S. J. & Bowman, M. (2000). *Beyond New Age: Exploring Alternative Spirituality*. Edinburgh: Edinburgh University Press.

Swets, J. & Bjork, R. (1990). Enhancing Human Performance: An Evaluation of "New Age" Techniques Considered by the U.S. Army. *Psychological Science*, 1(2), 85–96.

Taylor, C. (1989). *Sources of the Self: The Making of the Modern Identity*. Cambridge, MA: Harvard University Press.

Tipton, S. M. (1982). *Getting Saved From the Sixties: Moral Meaning in Conversion and Cultural Change*. Berkeley: University of California Press.

Tolkien, J. R. R. (1938 [2001]). On Fairy Stories. In *Tree and Leaf*. London: HarperCollins.

Tolkien, J. R. R. (1954 [1987]). *The Fellowship of the Ring*. Vol. I of *The Lord of the Rings*. Boston, MA: Houghton Mifflin.

Trilling, L. (1971). *Sincerity and Authenticity*. Cambridge, MA: Harvard University Press.

Troeltsch, E. (1992 [1912]). *The Social Teachings of the Christian Churches*, 2 vols. Louisville, KY: Westminster John Knox Press.

Turkle, S. (2002). Our Split Screens. *Etnofoor*, 15(1–2), 5–19.

Veenstra, A. & Kuipers, G. (2013). It Is Not Old-Fashioned, It Is Vintage: Vintage Fashion and the Complexities of 21st Century Consumption Practices. *Sociology Compass*, 7(5), 355–65.

Voas, D. & Chaves, M. (2016). Is the United States a Counterexample to the Secularization Thesis? *American Journal of Sociology*, 121(5), 1517–56.

Wallis, R. (1975). Scientology: Therapeutic Cult to Religious Sect. *Sociology*, 9(1), 89–100.

Wallis, R. (2003). Three Types of New Religious Movement. In L. L. Dawson, ed., *Cults and New Religious Movements: A Reader*. Malden, MA: Blackwell, pp. 36–58.

Ward, P., Coveney, J., & Henderson, J. (2010). A Sociology of Food and Eating: Why Now? *Journal of Sociology*, 46(4), 347–51.

Watts, G. (2022). *The Spiritual Turn: The Religion of the Heart and the Making of Romantic Liberal Modernity*. Oxford: Oxford University Press.

Watts, G. & Houtman, D. (2022). Purification or Pollution? The Debate over "Workplace Spirituality." *Cultural Sociology*, 16(4), 439–56.

Watts, G. & Houtman, D. (2024). Introduction: Spirituality – Privatized Pseudo-Religion? In D. Houtman & G. Watts, eds., *The Shape of Spirituality. The Public Significance of a New Religious Formation*. New York: Columbia University Press, pp. 1–37.

Weber, M. (1948 [1919]). Science as Vocation. In H. H. Gerth & C. W. Mills eds., *From Max Weber: Essays in Sociology*. London: Routledge, pp. 129–56.

Weber, M. (1978 [1921/22]). *Economy and Society: An Outline of Interpretive Sociology*, 2 vols., G. Roth & C. Wittich, eds. Berkeley: University of California Press.

Weber, M. (1993 [1963]). *The Sociology of Religion*. Boston, MA: Beacon Press.

Weber, M. (2005 [1904/05]). *The Protestant Ethic and the Spirit of Capitalism*. London: Routledge.

Wertheim, M. (2000 [1999]). *The Pearly Gates of Cyberspace: A History of Space from Dante to the Internet*. London: Virago Press.

White, A. D. (1960). *A History of the Warfare of Science with Theology in Christendom*, 2 vols. New York: Dover.

Wilson, B. (1985). Secularization: The Inherited Model. In P. E. Hammond, ed., *The Sacred in a Secular Age: Toward Revision in the Scientific Study of Religion*. Berkeley: University of California Press, pp. 9–20.

Winnick, T. A. (2005). From Quackery to 'Complementary' Medicine: The American Medical Profession Confronts Alternative Therapies. *Social Problems*, 52(1), 38–61.

Woodhead, L. (1993). Post-Christian Spiritualities. *Religion*, 23(2), 167–81.

Wuthnow, R. (1976). *The Consciousness Reformation*. Berkeley: University of California Press.

Wuthnow, R. (1998). *After Heaven: Spirituality in America since the 1950s*. Los Angeles: University of California Press.

Wuthnow, R. (2003). The New Spiritual Freedom. In L. L. Dawson, ed., *Cults and New Religious Movements: A Reader*. Malden, MA: Blackwell, pp. 89–112.

Yeffeth, G. (2003). *Taking the Red Pill: Science, Philosophy and Religion*. Dallas: Smart Pop Books.

York, M. (1995). *The Emerging Networks: A Sociology of the New Age and Neopagan Movements*. London: Rowman & Littlefield.

Zandbergen, D. (2011). New Edge: Technology and Spirituality in the San Francisco Bay Area. PhD dissertation, Institute of Cultural Anthropology and Developmental Sociology, University of Leiden, Leiden.

Zijderveld, A. (2000). *The Institutional Imperative: The Interface of Institutions and Networks*. Amsterdam: Amsterdam University Press.

# Acknowledgments

As the authors, we thank our talented student-assistant Amber Sels for her comments and support in editing the text and literature and Rebecca Moore – editor for the Elements in New Religious Movements series – for her valuable suggestions, meticulous reading, and final editing work.

# Cambridge Elements

## New Religious Movements

### Founding Editor

†James R. Lewis

*Wuhan University*

The late James R. Lewis was a Professor of Philosophy at Wuhan University, China. He was the author or co-author of 128 articles and reference book entries, and editor or co-editor of 50 books. He was also the general editor for the *Alternative Spirituality and Religion Review* and served as the associate editor for the *Journal of Religion and Violence*. His prolific publications include *The Cambridge Companion to Religion and Terrorism* (Cambridge University Press 2017) and *Falun Gong: Spiritual Warfare and Martyrdom* (Cambridge University Press 2018).

### Series Editor

Rebecca Moore

*San Diego State University*

Rebecca Moore is Emerita Professor of Religious Studies at San Diego State University. She has written and edited numerous books and articles on Peoples Temple and the Jonestown tragedy. Publications include *Beyond Brainwashing: Perspectives on Cultic Violence* (Cambridge University Press 2018) and *Peoples Temple and Jonestown in the Twenty-First Century* (Cambridge University Press 2022). She is reviews editor for *Nova Religio*, the quarterly journal on new and emergent religions published by the University of Pennsylvania Press.

### About the Series

Elements in New Religious Movements go beyond cult stereotypes and popular prejudices to present new religions and their adherents in a scholarly and engaging manner. Case studies of individual groups, such as Transcendental Meditation and Scientology, provide in-depth consideration of some of the most well known, and controversial, groups. Thematic examinations of women, children, science, technology, and other topics focus on specific issues unique to these groups. Historical analyses locate new religions in specific religious, social, political, and cultural contexts. These examinations demonstrate why some groups exist in tension with the wider society and why others live peaceably in the mainstream. The series highlights the differences, as well as the similarities, within this great variety of religious expressions.

# Cambridge Elements

# New Religious Movements

## Elements in the Series

*Mormonism*
Matthew Bowman

*Jehovah's Witnesses*
Jolene Chu and Ollimatti Peltonen

*Wearing Their Faith: New Religious Movements, Dress, and Fashion in America*
Lynn S. Neal

*Santa Muerte Devotion: Vulnerability, Protection, Intimacy*
Wil G. Pansters

*J. Krishnamurti: Self-Inquiry, Awakening, and Transformation*
Constance A. Jones

*Making Places Sacred: New Articulations of Place and Power*
Matt Tomlinson and Yujie Zhu

*Korean New Religions*
Don Baker

*The Revelation Spiritual Home: The Revival of African Indigenous Spirituality*
Massimo Introvigne, Rosita Šorytė

*Abuse in New Religious Movements*
Sarah Harvey

*Early Twentieth Century New Black Religious Movements in the United States*
Darrius D. Hills

*Minority Religions, the Law, and the Courts: Cases and Consequences*
James T. Richardson

*New Religious Movements and the Romantic Spirit of Modernity*
Stef Aupers, Dick Houtman and Galen Watts

A full series listing is available at: www.cambridge.org/ENRM

For EU product safety concerns, contact us at Calle de José Abascal, 56–1°, 28003 Madrid, Spain or eugpsr@cambridge.org.

www.ingramcontent.com/pod-product-compliance
Lightning Source LLC
LaVergne TN
LVHW020006080526
838200LV00081B/4386